T0193686

The
JOURNEY
of a
Sage

KRISTEN BOMAS

BALBOA.PRESS
A DIVISION OF HAY HOUSE

Balboa Press books may be ordered through booksellers or by contacting:

Balboa Press
A Division of Hay House
1663 Liberty Drive
Bloomington, IN 47403
www.balboapress.com
844-682-1282

Print information available on the last page.

ISBN: 979-8-7652-2630-8 (sc)
ISBN: 979-8-7652-2631-5 (e)

Library of Congress Control Number: 2022905232

Balboa Press rev. date: 06/10/2022

Contents

Introduction. vii

Preface: Understanding the Sage xi

Chapter 1   Why You Are Here 1

Chapter 2   Developing The Sage's Template™ 9

Chapter 3   The Template in Action 19

Chapter 4   Self—The Physical Experience 27

Chapter 5   Self—The Energetic Experience 55

Chapter 6   Using The Sage's Template™ to Master Your Life 63

Chapter 7   Speaking Your Truth—Embarking On Mastery 77

Chapter 8   Conclusion. 107

Appendix A 109

Introduction

It's been said in various incarnations through the years that we are the sum of our experiences. Author B.J. Neblett once wrote that, "like a flowing river, those ... experiences ... continue to influence and reshape the person we are, and the person we become."

How many of us, though, take the time to not only consider and process our experiences, but to unravel the deeper meaning inherent to life's vignettes? How many of us simply plow through life's challenges without trying to reveal truths about those episodes—truths that have the potential to liberate us?

If I've learned anything during my own journey, it's that the path of unfolding inner freedom is within everyone's reach. But that first step, a step made with pure intention and awareness of what lies ahead, is often the most difficult.

The Journey of a Sage not only will help you take that step, but it will open doors you never knew were closed. It will help you live beyond your fears and all that limits you. It will allow you to master your life instead of floundering in its shadows.

How do I know? For more than 20 years, I've incorporated a tool that's central to my practice and my teachings. The tool, which I named The Sage's Template™, was developed throughout my own healing and the healing of others. Time and again, I've had the honor of watching people use The Sage's Template™ to master their most crushing challenges, unveil their wisdom, and revel in the understanding it brings. All of us can heal in this life, but only if you're willing and open to it.

Of course, for some, that's easier said than done. Putting a mirror to one's experiences, especially difficult ones, can be daunting. Trust me, I know. There have been times in my own life when the pain felt all-consuming and too much to bear.

For much of high school, I had no sense of belonging. I felt ugly and, at times, worthless. Like many young women, I first defined myself through a man. But what started as a blind date in high school evolved into an abusive relationship by the time I was in college. It took the help of several friends to safely pull me out of that situation.

Even amid the worst times, something inside told me to follow the pain. I didn't understand why at first, and I wasn't yet ready to follow through on this almost primal instinct. But the feeling gnawed at me, especially as a later relationship—and decade-long marriage—ended during graduate school.

My divorce came on the heels of an incident in grad school that already had stirred my old insecurities. As part of my doctoral program, students were asked to participate in group therapy—but with a catch. Instead of one consistent therapist, professors with varying theoretical orientations were asked to lead the sessions. As an aspiring therapist, I found the process fascinating. I wanted more out of life—and more out of myself—and these different philosophies were pushing me beyond my comfort zone in a good way.

Then, one day in group therapy, a moment of candor sparked a turning point in my life. The professor that day asked the group how they felt about me. The class, in turn, seemed to speak as one: There were times when they didn't like me because they felt I was a know-it-all. The past had steamrolled into the present. The loneliness, the rejection, the absence of belonging—all of my deepest self-doubts came flooding back.

But something else happened that day and the days that followed. I followed the pain. I chose, willingly and with purpose, to lean into the uncomfortable reality of their perception. If I really wanted answers, I couldn't walk away from a moment like this. Was I a know-it-all? Because of my insecurities, I certainly felt like I had something to prove. And yes, I was a bright student. At the time, intelligence was what I thought I had to offer the world. Maybe, the students were right. Maybe, it was far more complicated. But I could live with it. More importantly, I wanted to learn from it.

And so it began. It started with a simple, humble acknowledgement. Even in a challenging moment, the opportunity for continuing education exists. If you're available to it. The more experiences I approached with that mindset, including the subsequent end to my marriage, the more doors that opened. The more I explored challenges by looking for the gifts within, the more I understood the truth of life unveiled.

Not long after graduate school, I started my private practice. My original practice was steeped psychoanalytic psychotherapy. But a few years in, my clients started asking different questions, questions that broke the ceiling of traditional psychology. They were curious about life beyond fear-based thoughts and surface-level feelings. It wasn't just, "Why did John cheat on me?"

It was, "Why am I involved in the same relationship over and over again?"

"How do I open up my relationships; they feel so limited."

"Where do I find happiness?"

My patients were leaning into their challenges, just I was in my life—and they were asking all the right questions. I soon found myself having access to answers. There was a synergy developing between my personal journey and my professional journey. Those early years with my patients helped to form the foundation of The Sage's Template™.

This book represents the core of my teachings. Often, life's truths are very simple, but the mastery of those truths requires us to walk toward the fire. All of us have inner wisdom just waiting to be tapped. But are we able to endure the pressure or the pain that comes with a life experience and find the deeper meaning of that episode? Furthermore, can you grow from it? And heal from it?

You can. And this book will help you discover how.

Lao Tse Tung (Laozi), Buddha, Christ and other enlightened souls knew that life mastery was attainable through willingness and belief. Indigenous people of many lands believed that injury and illness came from the internal imbalances with Self, Spirit, and Earth. They mastered life with the help of a medicine wheel.

The Sage's Template™ incorporates several familiar philosophies and teachings, minus the medicine wheel, and combines them into an accessible blueprint, one that allows you to stay in the present while learning from the past.

You'll begin to understand the purposes of different challenges in life. We'll explore your Soulful Self and the external "Other" factors that produce internal reactions. You'll gain insights into your physical experience and your energetic experience. You'll better understand love-based and fear-based emotions, and how those feelings are the language of the soul. You'll learn that being out of tune can lead to illumination, and that transcending fear allows you to live in the greater truth: love.

It's no secret that relationships define this lifetime, and communication defines relationships. The Template can lead to a style of communication that opens you to your soulful purpose, that guides you to growth in your relationships, as well as inner growth.

It's through communication with "Self" that you'll learn to define the experiences you wish to have. It's through the communication with Self that you will move through challenges and begin to love the company you keep. It's through the communication of Self that you will become more present and in "the now." As you begin to live with compassion for Self, you also will live with compassion for others. As you begin to explore your Self, you will learn to explore others. Through the knowing and loving of Self, you will move into the awareness of The One and the infinite.

If none of this makes sense yet, trust me, it will.

The Sage's Template™ is a tool that can assist you in growing beyond assumptions and expectations. It can guide you to the answers within that help you move beyond taking things personally. Imagine the empowerment that comes with being a confident observer of life—someone who can see an episode for what it is, feel it, process it, and, ultimately, find the wisdom in it—instead of someone who only reacts to an experience but never grows from it.

It's time to lose your fears and discover the healing freedom that comes with life mastery.

Let the journey begin.

Preface: Understanding the Sage

In its role as an aromatic and sacred plant, sage has healing properties that date back some 4,000 years. Archaeological findings suggest that the ancient Egyptians used sage as everything from an embalming agent in Pharaonic tombs to a cure for infertility. In biblical lore, the sage plant willingly blossomed for the Virgin Mary amid a close encounter with King Herod's soldiers, creating protective cover for Baby Jesus and his mother during their flight with Joseph to Egypt.

In the Middle Ages, sage became a cure-all for medicine men who used it, among other reasons, to rid the body of illnesses connected to demonic possession. Even today, we burn sage to purify spaces and clear negative energy.

Similarly, the human version of the word sage also has quite a history. In ancient Greece, the Seven Sages represented a group of 6th century B.C. philosophers, politicians and legislators known for their towering wisdom. In Chinese culture, Confucius was considered "the sage of sages." In Hinduism, philosophical and spiritual sages with insights into complete understanding and absolute truth are called "Rishis."

For the purposes of this book, and the journey on which we're about to embark, the Sage embodies elements of both the plant and the philosopher. It represents a sense of healing. It represents profound and liberating wisdom. Most importantly, the Sage represents the ultimate freedom in this life.

What exactly does that mean? And how does it all fit into The Sage's Template™? Let's first start with a more detailed description. While the Sage is not gender specific, of course, I'll refer to her as a "she" in this section.

I view the Sage this way:

- The Sage is articulate and communicates with both knowledge and wisdom. She is a spiritual teacher. She is the wise one who travels the path of enlightenment or mastery.

- The Sage lives life in a state of surrender, accepting and flowing with all that is along her path. She is not searching for the answers. The sage is without ego. She embodies an understanding that extends beyond the need to know. The sage simply exemplifies and expresses love and happiness.

- The Sage possesses a sense of humor devoid of sarcasm. Her humor is enjoyed by all. She is comfortable in her own skin. She humbly expresses her true nature, her truth of Self.

- The Sage embodies wisdom that the philosopher seeks. Socrates taught a dialogue style that enabled people to speak of their differences until they found the true nature (or truth) that lies beyond those differences. The philosopher possesses the self-awareness of lacking knowingness; the Sage, however, is wise and lives according to an ideal that transcends this plane and physicality.

- The Sage lives her life based upon her own inner experiences. She knows her experiences. She also is unattached to them—and yet not detached. Therefore, she is fully present.

- The Sage is beyond all that is external. She takes nothing personally. Nothing ever disturbs the peace of her soul. The Sage's virtue is consistent with, and in agreement with, nature and eternal nature.

- The Sage lives her life consciously. She remains conscious and mindful in all daily tasks and responsibilities. Periodically, she enjoys the usual pleasures and suffers the usual pains like anyone else. Yet the Sage is without anxiety or worry. She transcends suffering through an understanding that it's part of a path to greater pleasure and peace.

- A Sage's life is serene. She knows the dual nature of life and, through transcendence, the absence of that duality. Her focus is on the relationship with her Self, with Other (i.e. persons, all life, the Earth), and with the infinite. As a result, she is an observer of life—her own life, as well as an observer of other people's lives. She accepts that attachments, judgments, fear, and suffering are the counterparts to freedom, joy, love, and peace.

- The Sage embraces whatever happens to her because she knows free will offers us choice in this lifetime. Therefore, whatever happens is with great purpose. She knows that the secret of her happiness and contentment is through this acceptance of what is. She knows the experience she wishes to have. She allows the surrender to deepen.

- The Sage knows how to love. She also knows not to expect love. She expresses her Self without needing a response. She has no expectations.

- The Sage is beyond the fear of being judged, criticized or rejected. She loves and accepts her Self for all she is, and for all that life is.

- The Sage sees the answers embedded in this life. She knows that people can experience an absence of suffering because, as children, people experience that absence in their moments of wonder, joy and happiness. Therefore, the Sage knows the end of suffering is a possibility for everyone—and that the magic of life is there for all to savor.

- The Sage teaches that you go within your Self to transcend the externally imposed obstacles and challenges that prevent you from moving beyond the suffering. That transcendence is permanent in your heart and spirit.

Ultimately, each of you is seeking to live beyond fear and suffering. Each of you has the desire to be at peace with your own life and its purpose. The Sage teaches that suffering and fear are transcended when your consciousness awakens. The goal of this awakening is an ongoing process, an evolving lifestyle—not an endpoint or destination.

Because the Sage is not attuned to the judgments of others—and, instead, is living within her own experience—people seek her company. She radiates wisdom, compassion, kindness, tranquility, and a discernible sense of harmony—and people are drawn to it like a beacon of light.

It's no surprise, then, that people may seek her advice. Only when the advice is sought, does the Sage present her thoughts to others in a direct way. Even then, she is confident, humble, simple, and efficient in her offerings. Her ego does not exist to teach others. She has no expectations. She is compassionate, empathetic, and deeply knowing and understanding of the questioner's suffering.

Over the course of my life, I've been inspired by the Sage. And I aspire to be a Sage. I have learned, and continue to learn, to surrender to my wisdom and my life.

As you embark upon the teachings of this book, I'm confident that you will begin to discover the Sage within. And you will nurture that discovery. You will choose to master as much of this life's challenges as you choose through your own free will. The more you master, the closer you will become to being the Sage. Along the way, you'll learn, as I've learned, that the challenges presented in this life feel much less ominous once you understand the true direction of your journey.

May the Sage show us the way.

CHAPTER

1

Why You Are Here

It's not easy to see the bigger picture amid the vignettes that play out each day in our lives. How can we possibly consider life's eternal questions when the stresses at work feel all-consuming? Or when the bills are mounting? Or when a relationship begins to fray? Is that really the time to ponder the purpose of our existence?

It is, especially when you realize that the way we process our daily dramas is directly connected to that greater purpose.

Let me put it another way. What if I told you that the key to unlocking this larger philosophical question had everything to do with understanding the challenges you face and the choices you make? That you're here to heal the very hurdles that life presents.

Imagine understanding how your individuality—and all the choices that comprise it—influences the journey on which you embark? Imagine being so in tune with your experiences, your decisions, your reactions, your emotions—so aware of your true nature—that you're able to see life, and your role in it, in a way that's both liberating and empowering.

That's the path down which The Sage's Template™ will lead you. But let's not get ahead of ourselves. Let's go back to life and its purpose.

By and large, the experiences of this life are either fear-based (and uncomfortable), or love-based (and comfortable). Most everyone is looking to feel comfortable, to be in a "good" place. However, life isn't that easy. It's inevitable that you will experience fear, which, in turn, creates the illusion of separation. It's through the recognition and understanding of fear—and then the ability to transcend that fear (along with the pain that accompanies it)—that you're able to experience the truth of who you are.

To help illustrate this more clearly, I incorporate two parables into my teachings. They offer accessible examples that speak to life, its general purpose, and why we're meant to confront challenges. The two questions I'm most often asked are: What is the purpose of this life (parable No. 1)? And, what is the purpose of my life (parable No. 2)?

Remember, it's the mastery of your challenges that allows healing to occur. Let's begin.

Parable No. 1: Note C

What most of us commonly refer to as our spiritual soul comes from a place of pure energy. But that's not exactly a tangible description. Also, we've heard the line, "We are souls having a human experience." So, let's put it into the context of the purpose of life.

Imagine that the soul instead comes from an energy of sound, one harmonious chord comprised of infinite notes. Let's say that you are Note C. You're Note C because you've been told so, but you really know nothing other than the beautiful sound of the chord. You can't distinguish yourself from the greater whole. Then, one day, Note C is wildly off key for some reason. The entire chord screams, "Note C is out of tune! Note C is out of tune!"

"Oh, wait! That's me!" you say. Suddenly, you can discern the difference between "you" and the other notes.

Boom! Now, you are in this life. This life is you. Out of tune.

Take a second to consider what it feels like to be Note C in that moment—the sensation of being isolated and out of sync, of being unique and noticeable.

Conversely, imagine how good it must feel to hear Note C back in tune, how seamlessly it now blends in with the chord. You're aware of your individual presence as part of a greater whole, yet you also appreciate the feeling of unity when the chord is playing as one.

Life holds similar rhythms and discord. You are here to get back in tune. But like any note that's off-key, it may take multiple efforts to fine-tune it. This life is about the challenges or the out of tune. Soulfully, you are aware of how good it will feel to be part of the whole, but, physically, you will choose how much tuning to actually conquer. That is your free will.

Love-based emotions and experiences define the truth of who and what you are—and that allows you to plug in to the whole, or the "One." Fear-based emotions and experiences, on the other hand, create the sensation of feeling out of tune. And when you're out of tune, you may feel a sense of separateness from the whole.

But here's the rub. You're not separate at all. Much like Note C, you perceive the illusion of being separate. That allows you to feel your "identity," your energy signature, or your "Self" as a separate entity (*Note: We'll explore terms like "Self" and their relevance to the Template in Chapter 2*). Healing occurs as you successfully understand and heal life's challenges. That is the tuning process. As you heal, you become keenly aware of the essence or presence of you, the individual. You're also aware of being a part of The One.

To put it another way, you identify with your fears until you begin releasing them. When you are beyond all fear, you are left with only the truth of who you are.

Only then can you feel your Self as a unique energetic signature that is a part of the whole, The One. Not separate but part of. Not blended but unique. Not self but One. Ultimately, the soul is working to move through the fear-based experiences to find, define and feel its unique sense of the whole.

What does that mean exactly? It means that, soulfully, you're here to be tuned up.

Consequently, our journey on this plane is to do just that. To find truth beyond the fear that has left you off-balance, unmoored, and out of sync. The Sage's Template™ is designed to be a tool that you can use in everyday life to consciously begin this definition of truth.

Existing beyond all fear and as pure love is the truth of who we are—as individuals and as a collective species.[1]

PARABLE NO. 2: LIFE IS A PLAY

It should come as no surprise that life, in so many ways, can be a paradox. For example, your existence is utterly unique. Your life is unfolding in a way that's exclusive to you. And yet, at the same time, your life also is part of a far greater mosaic. Each day your individual life intersects with—and even becomes entwined with—other individual lives. You exchange pleasantries with the barista at Starbucks. A stranger cuts you off in traffic. You talk shop with a co-worker. A friend invites you to dinner. You compare days with your significant other.

Your personal journey—your thoughts, your emotions, your interactions, your decisions—is different than every other journey. In that sense, you stand alone. But it's not a one-person show. Your life is filled with an endless array of co-stars.

Let's run with that concept.

Pretend, as a soul, you're a playwright. You're writing an original story based on an imagined experience. You identify the lead character and what he or she will experience. You choose the time, the location, and specific backdrops. You select the main supporting characters—the mother, the father, the siblings, the best friends. They'll not only advance the plot, but they'll help manifest the experience that the main character is destined to have. What makes this play interesting is that you decide to let each actor improvise their part. Beforehand, you explain to the actors that they must somehow create situations for the main character to have specific experiences—but how they do that is up to them. Finally, you hire all of the secondary characters necessary to give scenes a slice-of-life feel.

Ultimately, you become the director of this play. As director, you're constantly revising scenes so that the drama feels true and accurate. In the end, you cast yourself as the main character.

---

[1] Love is a higher vibration than fear. This is what you have heard defined as higher dimensions. The evolution of this race is moving toward the experience of love as a higher vibration or dimension.

Each act is critical to the overall experience of the play. There's an opening act that offers a backstory for the main character, thus setting the stage for what's to come. Within the play, acts may produce a transformation in the character, offer moments of clarity, or produce an unexpected plot twist that still ties into the larger story.

The play, of course, is about your life and your relationships. This is your story unfolding. You are the main character. And the audience, in this case, is your higher Self, or the "soul" (which is always present to guide us).

In your play, you can see that the past is a necessary part of the story; it provides context for what's to come—and wisdom for those able to connect past to present. The present provides experiences that give you opportunities to heal the past and be fully conscious in the now. The future has yet to be designed (in part, because of the improvisation of your other characters).

The present is your only "reality." Just like in the play, the present scene is the only one being viewed and experienced by the audience. Yet it evokes emotion because of prior scenes. In your life, if you are currently suffering challenges or patterns from the past, you're not able to be present. Why? Because your thoughts and fear-based emotions are steeped in prior experiences. Therefore, during those fear-based moments, you are living in the past.

You are built upon everything that you experience. Thus, your challenges are an integral part of your unique purpose in this life. You either will master those challenges or you won't. When you do master a challenge, you're no longer mired in your past. Instead, you build upon the freedom that comes with healing.

Life, indeed, is like a play. It has purpose and meaning. And there are identifiable themes that you're able to summarize when explaining the story. When describing the essence of a play (or a movie) to a friend, you may say that it was a great romance filled with unconditional love. It was about courage and perseverance. It was about how good conquered evil. It was about self-destructive loss and redemption.

Your life, as well, can be summed up by an identifiable theme. Significant periods are often explained this way. For example, think about your high school years. Take a minute to sum up your high school experience and what it meant to you. Write it down. It's only a few sentences, right? Four years of your life are condensed into a brief description. Still, that description possesses considerable meaning. It provides an insight into how that experience shaped your life—and your definition of Self. Ultimately, your life journey will be summed up with a brief description based on your overall experience. It's that description that holds the key to your purpose on this plane.

A few final thoughts on life as a play.

Keep in mind that all the secondary characters in your play of life are the writers and directors of their own plays—and that you're a secondary character in their stories. It's mind-blowing to consider how all of these lives, which seem so separate, are so interconnected. But that's life.

Let's look at an example of a secondary character, a partner in your life. This person is the main character of his/her own life play. Their stage is on one side of the theater; your stage is on the other. If you are in a relationship where you are constantly focusing on this other person—and doing everything he/she wants you to do—you have left your own stage. You're spending your time on their stage. Think about that. We'll revisit this idea soon.

Remember, life is not predestined. You have free will, as do all of your characters. As the director, writer, and lead character of your play, you have the power to rewrite a scene, say goodbye to a character, or hold steady with the story. This is your play, and it's playing out as your life.

With that in mind, there's no time like the present to think about how you want each scene to end. It's your choice. Never forget that.

THE PURPOSE OF CHALLENGES IN THIS LIFE

As you can see from the parables, you're going to have challenges in this life. This is by design. They're here to help you unveil your truth. In Note C, being out of tune represents the challenges of this life, and "tuning" is symbolic of mastering those challenges.

So, where do the challenges come from?

From the time you're able to start perceiving, challenges begin forming. Challenges are "learned" in this life from all other components of your experiences. From your late second trimester in utero, you began perceiving the world around you. From birth until about age 22, you grow by leaps and bounds—physically, emotionally, intellectually, intuitively, spiritually. In those years, you are constantly changing—and your world is constantly changing. You are, consequently, perceiving life uniquely.

Those unique perceptions are the bricks upon which your life is built. The people, systems, culture, society, and more (*known as "Other," which will be explored in Chapter 2*) are putting upon you all they think you require to shape your life. The contrasts or conflicts that occur between what is put upon you and the truth of who you are define and construct your challenges. (*Note: These life experiences are addressed in greater detail in Chapter 4.*)

This life will set in motion, through challenges and experiences, all that you need to heal and to unveil your truth. How far you go in that pursuit is entirely up to you. You have free will. You may decide to master a challenge or to suffer with it. The challenges are put in place only for you to overcome them.

Because the challenges in life are built from fear-based experiences, they house your fear-based emotions. These emotions, in turn, explain why you take things personally or why you're defensive. Consequently, your communication is going to be influenced by your challenges and the challenges of others. The Sage's Template™ addresses the simplicity of challenges versus truth in the mastery of life. The path of mastery, as we've already noted, is about transcending your fears. More on this soon.

Onward.

2

Developing The Sage's Template™

Ideally, most of you want to live each day with awareness and intent. You're here for a purpose—to have a soulful experience as a human being. But as you're beginning to learn, it's not easy to master the present—or see the future—without first understanding your past.

Let's explore that.

Your early development set the stage for you through your unique experiences and perceptions. Upon birth, you were taught to think, believe, behave, and exist based on what other people, and what society, expected of you. So, how does this foundational period of your life, one steeped in external forces, somehow lead to revelations about your true self?

The Sage's Template™ is designed to allow you to stay in the present while using the past to heal challenges, as was mentioned in the previous chapter.

Let's start by developing the Template.

Here is you today (Figure 1).

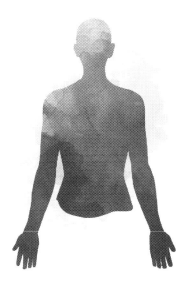

Let's add to this entity your **Soulful Self** (Figure 2).

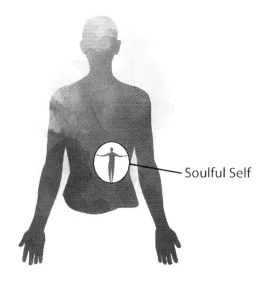

What is the Soulful Self? Think of it as your true nature. This is who and what you really are. Your Soulful Self understands, appreciates, and nurtures your purpose on this plane. It includes the unique and open self that existed upon entering this life. It also includes your intuition and your connection to all that is. So, if this small oval in the illustration is the ultimate truth that you are here to reveal, what comprises the rest of "you?"

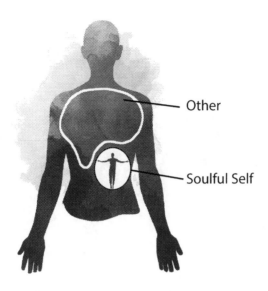

Moving forward, the external input in life will be referred to as **Other** (Figure 3). Other is defined by family, friends, society, culture, experiences, and systems that influence your formative years. As it pertains to the Template, Other will be used to describe limitations instead of growth. Think of it as a dark stormy day. From your position, all you can see and experience are the dark clouds; you can't see the sun. But if you can break the clouds apart, you will find the sun, in all of its glory, shining brightly on the other side. It's the dark stormy clouds that restrict the potential of the soulful self. It's the sun that is the Soulful Self. Is it possible that a family member or friend can be unconditionally loving and accepting of you? Absolutely. But when that doesn't happen—when Other represents impediments and suppression—dark clouds are created by these external influences. This makes it challenging for the Soulful Self to shine (or present) as your truth.

Let's take this idea a step further (Figure 4).

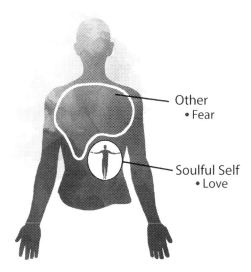

The Soul comes into this existence from a place and energy of *love*. In its true essence, the Soulful Self is of love. Other, meanwhile, puts *fear* upon you.

In life, there are very few truths. The Sage's Template™ exposes two of them (Figure 5):

1) Fear is always *illusion*.
2) Love is always *truth*.

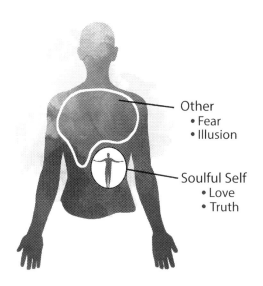

Looking at Figure 5, from which pocket do you think most of your language comes when you are speaking? Is it the big pocket or the little one? For most people, it's the Other pocket (Figure 6).

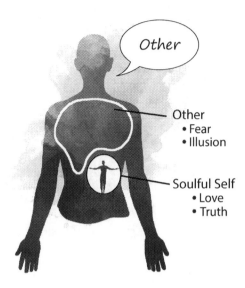

And yet, you believe you're speaking from the heart, from the Self. For that reason, I call this **SelfOther** language (Figure 7). It's language that you took on from Other.

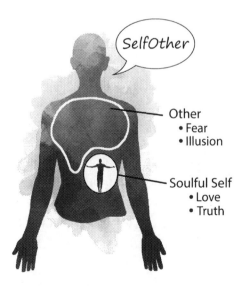

To find your truth in this life, you must be able to separate Self from Other.

To do this, I will use **your language**—spoken, thoughts, and imagined—as the source for healing and change. Your language is with you always, and so you can learn to listen to your Self. Your language will teach you what your challenges are and how they are presenting. That language also will tell you what emanates from the truth of Self, and what stems from Other teachings. This begins your awareness of Self versus Other.

By separating Self versus Other, you are separating Truth versus Illusion and Love versus Fear (Figure 8).

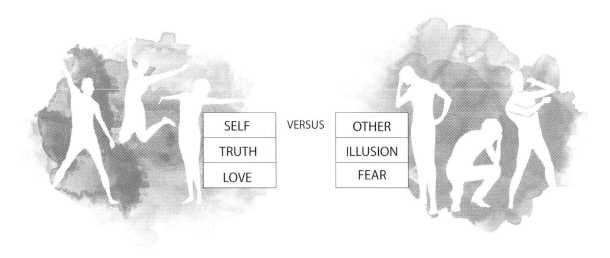

At first, you may feel that it's counterintuitive to separate Self from Other when you are told that we are all one. Yet, in order to embrace and experience that oneness, it's imperative to move beyond the illusion of separateness. That happens within you. It is in the Soulful Self that you will find the experience of One. For some people, meditation may unlock this door—because in meditation you are moving beyond the external and into the infinite of the internal.

In Figure 8, I simplified your physical life into a dualistic model. The duality of life is how you learn in this life: You know there is an outside *because* there is an inside; you know there is a left *because* there is a right. Love is the absence of fear, and fear is the absence of love. They cannot co-exist. When you're feeling angry at someone, you cannot simultaneously feel love for them. You can love them *before* and *after* you feel angry—but not at the same time.

Figure 8 represents your physical life, but there are two aspects to this life: physical and energetic. The circle that encompasses the Soulful Self represents both aspects. The model, therefore, must address the energy, or Soul (Figure 9), that defines this existence.

If the physical self speaks a SelfOther language, then the Soul must also have a language. And if the Soul is energy, it stands to reason that its language also must be energy. Therefore, the language of the Soul is emotion.

Emotions are also dualistic. There are **Love-Based** and **Fear-Based** emotions (Figure 10).

LOVE-BASED	FEAR-BASED
Love	Fear
Joy	Anger
Surrender	Hurt
Unity	Lonely
Harmony	Guilt
Peace	Shame
Tranquility	Attachment
Acceptance	Abandonment
Etc.	Etc.

So, now, let's put it all together. Look at Figure 11 on page 17. This is The Sage's Template™. It's the culmination of everything that has been discussed so far. This is the chart to which I'll be referring as I talk about finding freedom in your life.

The left-hand side of the Template is the description of all you wish to experience in life. The upper section describes the physical experience, and the lower part defines where you are soulfully and spiritually connected. This is the Soulful Self in its physical and energetic state. It's the truth of who and what you are. This is the place where you feel expansive, open, and free. Throughout the rest of the book, I will periodically call this the Truth Pocket.

The right column of the Template, meanwhile, defines the challenges of this life. This is the side that illuminates that which can be mastered or transcended (as you choose). These are the challenges put upon you by Other during the foundational period of your life. It's that which makes you feel small, trapped, and limited.

Consequently, I will interchangeably call this the Other pocket or the Challenge pocket. Your challenges define your purpose because that's where you are "out of tune."

So, let's tune you up by turning to everyday life—and seeing how to put the Template to use.

Figure 11: The Sage's Template™

LOVE-BASED	FEAR-BASED
Love	Fear
Joy	Anger
Surrender	Hurt
Unity	Lonely
Freedom	Guilt
Acceptance	Shame
Peace	Attachment
Harmony	Abandonment
Etc.	Etc.

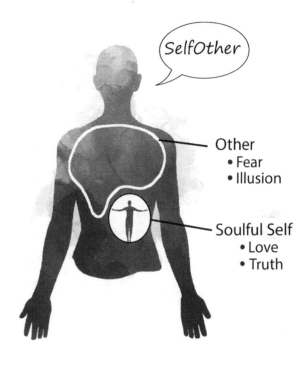

CHAPTER

·

3

·

The Template in Action

As fans of the *Star Wars* franchise can attest, not all sages present as human. But that doesn't mean their words can't hold truth. In *The Empire Strikes Back*[2], part of the original trilogy of *Star Wars* movies, Luke Skywalker encounters Yoda. At one point, the Jedi Master explains to young Skywalker that, "You must unlearn all you have learned to know The Force. The energy that is between … unites all of us through its luminous threads. You must feel the energy."

Yoda's wisdom also applies to The Sage's Template™. As we explored in the previous chapter, the Template offers a path to freedom and abundance. Through a deep understanding of your own experience, it's possible to heal the fear-based restrictions that you wish to remove from this life.

However, discerning those experiences, as Yoda would suggest, requires you to embrace something that may seem counterintuitive at first. Until now, you've learned primarily from external sources that interrupt your true expression of Self. With help from the Template,

---

[2] *Star Wars: Episode V —The Empire Strikes Back* (1980) Lucas Film Ltd., USA

you're going to *move into your feeling of the experience.* You're going to push beyond your fear and doubt, the impediments to your freedom, and stand in belief of all that you can be. Once you understand the energy of life, you'll understand how you manifest all that is around you.

The Template uses the simplicity of the duality in this physical life to initiate your healing, so that you move beyond fear. Ultimately, it can lead to a "mastery" style of living that opens you to freedom within your Self—and an understanding of your Soulful Self. If you choose, it can help you move beyond the duality of this life.

If all of this seems a bit daunting, don't worry. We're about to make practical use of the Template.

Let's start by identifying an experience in your current life that's on your mind. Maybe it's an episode connected to work, or family, or a relationship. Now, review the two columns on the left side of The Sage's Template™ (Figure 11)—love-based emotions and fear-based emotions. If the present-day experience that comes to mind is uncomfortable, then you're experiencing fear-based emotions (in the right column). See if you can pinpoint specific emotions connected with the discomfort. If so, great. If you don't see your fear-based emotion in Figure 11, turn to Appendix A (in the back of the book); there are dozens of additional fear-based emotions. Find the one (or ones) that resonate when you think about this experience. After picking out the emotions, ask yourself when you last felt them.

Once you identify that memory, try and recall the feelings attached to it. Let them wash over you and ask, again, when you last felt that way. Keep looking back and asking yourself when you previously felt that set of emotions until you feel you've reached an oldest memory.[3]

> *Example 3.1.* A couple, Sam and Tony, had been dating for a while. Periodically, Sam would accuse Tony of not loving him. Tony was confused; he consistently felt unheard and untrusted by Sam's accusations. As they learned to communicate, Sam was able to realize that, throughout his life, he had a fear of love and good times coming to an abrupt, hurtful end.

---

[3] Unveil Your Truth: 6 Steps to Moving beyond Limiting Beliefs. This is a small ebook that takes you through the six steps of dismantling old beliefs and their corresponding judgments. This little book helps you with all the steps necessary to begin the process of separating Self from Other.

At those times, Sam felt what he described as a "cruddy" fear inside. He wasn't sure from where it came. He was able to use the fear-based emotions list (Appendix A) to name quite a few emotions attached to the remembered experience. From there, he identified a memory prior to that memory where he felt the same. He continued that process back to an early childhood recollection. In the process, he was able to identify several teachings from early childhood that led to him being fearful of an unannounced retraction of love and understanding.

By doing this with Tony, they were both able to understand why the thoughts were there. Tony no longer took it personally. The relationship opened its communication in a way that allowed them to become closer rather than farther apart.

Once you are at the oldest memory, you are ready to move up to the top of the Template and explore Truth versus Illusion. Tease apart the oldest memory to see what you were doing prior to the discomfort. Once you identify that, you have shown your Self that you were doing something *you wanted to do* when a force of tumult or disruption came in and prompted the fear-based experience. You can now identify what is truth and what is illusion. Truth is what you were doing prior; illusion is what was put upon you.

Now, let's connect this to Self and Other. By identifying your truth prior to the upsetting interruption, you have identified Self. You were doing something that *you chose to do*, something that probably was giving you some sort of happiness. The interruption is Other, *the external influence that sent you into fear-based feelings*. Other had its own set of perceptions and beliefs, and that sent your happy space into turmoil.

Once you have taken the oldest memory and dissected it into Self versus Other, it's time to begin the healing. Try meditating on the earliest event; the goal is to observe the full memory of you in yesteryear. In addition to being the present-day observer in the meditation, you also want to feel your Self *as the child*, experiencing the entire memory from pleasant to painful.

In the memory, were you happy, innocent, focused? Know how you felt leading up to the fear-based event. What was your true experience prior to the point when Other added fear to the situation? As the child, see if you also can be an observer of those around you.

As you begin to master your life experiences through use of The Sage's Template™, you will begin to view episodes like this through three prisms: you, as you are in the present; you, in yesteryear, as you were in the full memory of your past; and you, in yesteryear, but as the observer of other.

Let's use the example of Sam.

> **Example 3.2.** In Sam's oldest memory, he was about 6 years old. He was playing in his room with a friend. He was having a great time and was focused on the game. Suddenly, his mother came into the room and yelled at him. She had been calling him for dinner, and he hadn't responded. She grew angry, she halted the game, and she yelled at Sam's friend to go home. Sam was pleading for her to let them finish the game, but she said no. He felt the shame of his friend being yelled at and "kicked out" out of the house. Sam felt like he had done something wrong, but he didn't know what. He swore he would be more aware of his mom calling for him. The vagueness of the episode and "what he did wrong" solidified his need to be good enough—and solidified his fear of not being good enough.
>
> Then there was his mother's side, which was a complete unknown to him. Let's imagine she had a long and difficult day. Perhaps, she didn't realize that he had closed his door and couldn't hear her. When he didn't respond to her calls, Sam's mother became increasingly irritated. By the time she climbed the stairs and reached his room, her frustration over everything that had happened that day boiled over. She opened the door and exploded. Maybe she just wanted to get dinner over with so she could relax.

In the example, you can see that Sam did *nothing* wrong. His mother was having her own experience. As a child, however, he had no other way to perceive the situation except to feel like it was *his fault*, that he did something to upset her. So, he took her anger personally. The outcome of that event led to a pain that stayed with Sam; it became a foundational episode. His mother, meanwhile, may have thought nothing of it as she served dinner. Or, perhaps, she felt bad about the overreaction—but never expressed that to Sam.

Teaching Moment. Let's stop here for a second. This story is an example of why it's crucial to give yourself the freedom to *pay attention to your own memories without judgment as to whether they are "right" or "wrong."* Don't worry about Other at this point. Take care of you, first. You'll be able to see exterior influences more clearly only after you understand your own past. You are built upon your perceptions and experiences, whatever they may be!

Now let's go back to the Template.

After you have discerned Self versus Other in your own old memory, come back to the present and reflect on the event. In your reenactment of that memory, you will see the innocence of your participation in the event. You will see how your happiness (or whatever feelings your episode involved) was interrupted by something that was completely foreign to your experience. That is the *illusion of fear.*

You absorbed the incident as if you did something wrong. It was a vague wrongness, so the vagueness increased the fear. Once you see that you were in your own creative world—one that was brutally interrupted without warning or reason—you can see that Other was a separate storyline, having a separate experience.

The two stories may have merged, but you are separate from Other.

Think about that. Let it sink in. *You are separate from Other.*

When you understand that, you're able to feel the innocence and happiness through the event. You do not take the interruption and comments personally. You even can go one step further and hear your Self comforting yourself. You see Other as handling it poorly, not you.

We're not there yet. But this where we're heading, with help from the Template. It's a seismic, life-altering shift in your Self and how you process the past and present. When you get to a place where you can recognize and utilize this shift, you are having what we call *a recapitulative experience.* As a result, you can feel the healing move through you.

The example also shows how your fear-based emotions and experiences develop. You can see how you begin this life entwined in the experiences of your parents and of Other. This is how your Self becomes buried during your early and formative years. By learning to feel the difference between the love- and fear-based emotions and experiences, you are opening the gateway to healing. Hopefully, through this example, you can see the importance of being able to feel and identify emotions in response to Other. This is where you begin your exploration in search of Self.

It will be helpful for you to use this information when you feel a brief challenge and the fear-based emotion(s) associated with it. In that moment, you can say:

"This is an illusion to help me feel the truth of my Self."

"This is an external experience that is showing me that I am not this!"

That acknowledgment will lead you to *journey into the challenge*, instead of away from it, to discover what lies on the other side. You may not always need to go through the steps listed above. There will come a time when you are familiar enough with your Soulful Self that you identify the experience and then shift. The Template, in this case, is helping you get started.

There are some fears that are very constant in your life. For example, you may believe worry is important to your relationship with life and your relationships in life. You may believe worrying motivates you. This, too, is all illusion.

You are motivated, in truth, to *get away* from the worry or fear because you are motivated to *be* free and to *find* success, pleasure, and reward. As you begin to realize your fears are illusion, you begin to look for your truth. Truth always will be found in love-based experiences—and will always give you joyful experiences. Truth, indeed, does set you free.

It's in the physical experiences (versus the energetic experiences) that you will unravel the Self from Other. You will see how the language of experience is going to be important in the process of mastery. As you begin to feel and clarify your inner thoughts, you will be able to move beyond this physical language and into a soulful language that comes from your wisdom. That growth will be paralleled by an experiential growth that can transcend the duality.

By removing the shackles of old beliefs, you can process and move beyond your fear-based emotions. At that point, you begin to feel a greater love and acceptance of your Self. That's when you begin to open the gateway to the Soulful Self and its truth.

Communication with your Self is the core to all communication and relationships. Once you know what is going on inside, you can teach other people in your life what that is. With that level of open communication, you can open your relationships to new levels of growth, love and acceptance.

Now that we've explored the periphery, let's do a deep dive into the components of The Sage's Template™.

CHAPTER

4

Self—The Physical Experience

INTRODUCTION

Can you identify feelings in your body? Do you recognize when your body is out of balance and stressed? Are you aware of your inner experience—or are you more attuned to external expectations, ones that you're eager to meet? Do you understand the beliefs you truly have? Or are you still holding onto what you were told to believe?

These are all questions tied in different ways to the physical experience of this life—that which the body physically feels and senses. It is this part of The Sage's Template™ that addresses your physical experience with Self and Other—where Love is Truth and Fear is Illusion, respectively. It's only in this physical existence that you feel separate and have the need to separate your Self from Other. That's because it is inside you that you find truth, transcend duality, and merge with The One. To do that, however, it's important that you're able to feel and know your physical Self.

So, what exactly does that entail as it pertains to the journey we're exploring?

You experience this life through what is happening around you and in you. Initially, those experiences are separate: outer and inner, respectively. You experience the external physical life as separate and dualistic. You perceive all that is around you with your unique awareness. You can interact with this physical life using your intellect and ego (external definitions) or your wisdom and truth (internal knowing).

It's your heart (soulful mind) that opens you to acceptance and forgiveness. But it's your physical mind that creates fear of the external—which, in turn, limits you and your freedom. In The Sage's Template™, external influences and experiences are those that *Other* puts upon you through *fear*. Subsequently, this created *illusions* for you to move beyond. For example, you may fear aggression or judgment from Other, and that may drive you to be perfect. Your thoughts may lead to choices that limit or alter your behavior—simply to meet the expectations of Other. There is much that can influence your freedom, and it's important to understand that it is (or was) all external to you.

You also have an inner experience of the external world. How you feel and interpret this life is unique to you. Within that inner experience are the external definitions and the internal knowing. The internal knowing is the true inner awareness of life, beyond the fear and external teachings that were put upon you. It's that inner place where you *know your truth*, feel *love and acceptance*, and experience true *Self.*

As sketched in the Template, Self, truth and love are who you are from when you entered the world; it's the outcome of your inner growth beyond the challenges of this life.

How, then, does the Other pocket develop? Let's revisit your past and explore why your story of origin is so important to your life journey.

DEVELOPMENT OF YOUR UNIQUE INNER EXPERIENCE

The past is never far from your present. For the purposes of The Sage's Template™, and the search for true Self, there's much to unpack in that sentiment. We're all built on our past; it's where we learn our challenges. And challenges, as we've discussed, are what define your specific purpose in this life.

To rise above these hurdles, to stop taking things so personally, it's important to understand why you developed the way you did—and how it influences who you are.

When you were born into this life, you were predominantly a sensory being. You could see, feel, hear, smell, taste, and, most of all, intuit experiences. Physically, your environment had transformed. You had transitioned from a dark, fluid-filled womb to a light, air-filled world. You went from a cocooned environment to an open unknown.

This was your first "death" experience, a transition where one experience ends (dies) to allow another to begin (born). Immediately after entering this world, you also felt abandonment (absence of mother) until you were placed in your birth mother's arms. This was your first experience of separation. That delay, which may have been prolonged based on medical circumstances, ignites the following experience: If you do not find your mother, you will die. Once reconnected with your mother, you become calm and attach to the safety and temporary absence of fear.

This demonstrates how life begins with the presence of fear or fear-based emotion.

There is considerable evidence[4] to suggest that you were aware of your energy self (soul), its entry into this life, and your purpose coming into this life. You even recall the beat of your mother's heart and the emotions she felt as a part of your memory of the womb experience. You knew "Mom" from the inside!

While most infants stayed with their birth mom, some were adopted by a separate set of parents, or maybe there was a surrogate mom.[5] Regardless, the memories at 1 week included all of the memories from the womb. Your memories at 3 weeks included everything from the first weeks. Your memories at 2 months included your memories of the third week and forward, and so on. Consequently, you are built on your experiences and memories—from this life and beyond.

---

[4]   Much of this research comes from hypnosis. The individual under hypnosis goes back to the womb and then can "see" or feel the soulfulness of their entry and can "know" the purpose or what they brought into this life. There are many spiritual teachers who talk about the soul being present prior to conception and that the parent(s) can feel the presence. There are various regressions both conscious and unconscious that have been documented where the individual knows their purpose or confronts their purpose in this life. I have a client who had a near-death experience. While on the other side, she was told by her guides that she was on this Earth to do and master certain experiences—and that it was very important that she do so. She was given direction and then "sent" back to get on track. This experience allowed her to know the challenges of darkness that she had been experiencing prior to the experience with her guides. She was able to let go of her fear/terror and move into her truth.

[5]   Your memories, consequently, will include the transition from birth's abandonment to a new set of parents. That is a different set of abandonment experiences in the first days (or years) of life.

Let's further the understanding of those foundational experiences by using an example of sight. At birth, you had approximately 8 inches of vision—the distance from a parent's cradled arm or breast to the parent's down-turned face. At that point, you didn't realize that anything existed in this physical world beyond what you could see. Therefore, your perception of the physical world had an 8-inch radius and was constantly changing. The most consistent experience was your primary parent and their face. Although your distance vision developed rapidly, your depth perception did not fully develop until approximately 7 months.

Your awareness that things existed outside of your vision did not develop until somewhere between the ages of 2 and 3. Therefore, your perceptions of the physical world around you were *completely unique*. Because you are built upon those perceptions, your experience of life always will be unique from everyone else's.

During those early years, your world was like pure magic. As an infant, when you felt hunger, you'd cry—and your primary parent would appear with food! Your parents were omnipotent and omnipresent. But your helpless state, further limited by your inability to understand that a world existed beyond what you could see, became the source of attachment to your primary parent. You instinctively knew that if you were abandoned, you would die.

As time went on, your developing perceptions continued to be unique—that is, until around age 22, when the last of your logical mind developed. You are built upon your perceptions. Consequently, your world remains perceptually unique to you in this lifetime.

Now, you understand that you came into this physical life with a purpose and a set of unique perceptions. These are core components of your life. From the inside looking out, the world is viewed as unique to you.

Next, let's look at the outside or external experience.

THE EXTERNAL EXPERIENCE OF SELF

The external world fuels your perception of time and space on this plane. As the participant or observer in this life, the external world has its own feel and look to you. Remember, you learned to use expectations and assumptions to experience the external world. Therefore, as you impose expectations or assumptions, the external world takes on a particular meaning that is yours. If there are old, learned beliefs within you, then your perceptions of the external world can be further skewed as an experience (or to hold meaning) within you.

The external world also is in a constant state of change. Each of you perceives the external in your own way. Therefore, the external world is not fixed *but illusive*. Together, it is a confound of the changing world and your changing perceptions. This is why "facts" can cause problems with communication in intimate relationships. Two people can perceive the same facts in completely different ways. Similarly, one person's actions or behaviors can stem from a particular intention—but can be received and interpreted with an opposite meaning by another person.

As people focus on the external, they leave the Self behind. This leaves the Self vulnerable. Because the focus is on everyone or everything around you, an experience can easily ignite a challenge.

> **Example 4.1.** A few generations of pugs ago, I had a pug who loved to bark at and chase the maintenance golf cart on the other side of the canal. As soon as he saw the cart, he would run to the back of the patio and bark at the golf cart as it drove across the property. Unfortunately, he was so focused on the external cart that he did not see the clay pots of plants in his path—and he'd inevitably run into a pot.

When you are focused on an external stimulus or event, you leave your inner self vulnerable to influence or attack. This is particularly true with addiction/alcoholism. If an addict can't learn to know their inner Self, they are constantly threatened by the substance of choice sneaking its way back into their life. There have been several times in my career where I've had clients call me in a panic because they found themselves in front of their dealer's house. They'd say, "I don't know how I got here!" In those cases, I've asked them where the nearest store is—and then I've met them in that parking lot to redirect their recovery. This is how insidious the challenges of your life can be.

The external experiences create and nourish *fear* and *illusion* that *Other* put upon you in this life. It's just a stage set. Like the parable (Life is a Play) in Chapter 1, the true "story" is the one that unveils within you on this staged play—and that play is about YOU.

THE INTERNAL EXPERIENCE OF SELF

The internal experience of you is the most important part of life. It is inside you where you learn to discern what is the *truth of you* versus what Other *put upon you*. Both pockets are inside you. It's why we talk with a SelfOther language.

Internally, you may know your Self in some ways but not others. You may know exactly what you wish to experience, or you may not. Even if you know what you wish to experience, you may not be able to hold onto that experience when another person influences you in his or her direction.

Thus, it's crucial in this life to discern what was put upon you and what is of you.

Let me share a story that illustrates this point. It speaks to how, once you learn to discern the difference between Self and Other, you can voice the truth of your experience.

> *Example 4.2*. Years ago, I was in the car with a man who I was dating at the time; we were driving back from breakfast. He was telling me *all about me*—what I think and what I do. I told him that his comments and thoughts were not me, and I attempted to tell him who I was. He interrupted and continued. Apparently, he had created an entire relationship around his assumptions of a person that did not exist within me. I felt no need to defend myself because he was describing something he had created from his own perceptions, assumptions and history (this is how the external world gets perceived so vastly). I told him that he didn't really need me in the seat next to him—because he was having a full relationship with a woman that was in his mind. "When you'd like to have a relationship with the woman next to you, rather than the one in your mind," I said to him, "let me know." It took him awhile to understand the significance of my comment.

Beliefs and perceptions are anchored in your history and therefore unique to you in many ways. Beliefs are an integral part of your internal experience. As you grow up, beliefs are imparted that, over time, feed into your limitations rather than your freedom. You may be conscious of some of those beliefs and unconscious of others. You may or may not have questioned some of these *taught* beliefs. Either way, you bought into them. All of these beliefs, memories, teachings, and more, are assimilated within you. They are important aspects of how you perceive this life—*but they are not of you in truth*. They are part of the "Other" pocket.

> ***Example 4.3.*** Many women have bought into the cultural belief about physical appearance. A beautiful woman with whom I worked (Sally) grew up with a parent who would constantly comment on her hair and appearance. Once she was of age, her parent would take her to the makeup specialists you see at department stores. The parent felt shame—and imparted that shame to Sally—when Sally's appearance was somehow deemed less than ideal by her parent. That shame became actively limiting when Sally bought into the parent's beliefs. She wasn't pretty enough. It didn't help that American culture and its emphasis on physical beauty played into this narrative. As Sally entered into relationships, she suffered from serious self-esteem and confidence issues—because she never felt good enough. She was beautiful inside and outside, but she couldn't see it. Not yet. But she would once she began to understand the taught belief that had been placed upon her.

As you become more focused (and eventually mindful) of your internal physical body, you will be more able to identify changes to the internal world of Self. This is important. All of life occurs within you. The Sage's Template™ will help you define the internal experience. From there, you can discern what is truth and wisdom within you—and what is illusion that was put upon you.

Once you gain that awareness, you can use the Template to begin the healing and transcendence of your challenges and past.

KNOWING YOUR INNER EXPERIENCE

As you begin to unveil your Self, start with a simple but clear identification of which emotions/feelings you are experiencing in the present experience: fear-based or love-based (See Figure 11 on page 17.)

Keep it simple. Are you uncomfortable (fear-based) or comfortable (love-based)? Once you have a general awareness of which side of the chart your feelings lie, begin specifying what you are feeling. Developing this emotional language is important; these feelings speak to your experiential world. For example, if yellow is your favorite color, it's your favorite *because* of the way it affects you or makes you feel.

By understanding the difference between fear-based and love-based emotional experiences, you know whether you're dealing with a challenge to Self or to the truth of Self, respectively. You can be aware of your Self in each life experience. This keeps you present to the current experience and allows you to be aware of your current inner experience.

When you find your Self having a fear-based experience, you know you're in your Other pocket—and that a challenge (from the past) has surfaced. You realize that you're experiencing limitations in life. If you are experiencing a fear, you have a choice to heal, ignore, or react to that experience.

When you find your Self having a love-based experience, you know you are experiencing truth of Self. You feel free and expansive—and you can build on that.

The more you are willing to explore challenges (fear) and learn to release them, the more you're open to your truth and Self (love). The more you experience your Self, free from the suffering, the greater your acceptance of Self, and the more you will enjoy your Self. From there, knowing your experience becomes easier.

Your physical self is a separate experience from other people, events, institutions, and experiences. The Template uses language, in particular your language, to allow you to begin separating Self from Other (external teachings), as well as Truth from Illusion, and Love from Fear.

Let's focus now on those three parts of the Template.

LOVE VERSUS FEAR

As you have already learned, love is the absence of fear, and fear is the absence of love. Therefore, the truth of Self is in absence of fear, and the illusion of Other is in absence of love.

This does not mean your parents, or those around you, didn't love you. It means that as fear was being imparted, love was not simultaneously felt. As previously stated, life is designed so that the fear put upon you creates the feeling of being separate (so that, ultimately, you can define Self from beyond fear). Remember, the "out-of-tune" experience in our parable about Note C (Chapter 1)? When Note C was out of tune, it felt "separate" from the one chord.

DISCERNING YOUR EXPERIENCE

Everything you experience in your life can be felt. All humans have the same set of emotions. As individuals, we feel those emotions based on different stimuli or experiences. To begin your understanding of Self, you first want to know if you are experiencing something comfortable or uncomfortable, love or fear, respectively.

Your overall life goal is probably to have as many good, happy experiences as possible. Yet, if you go back to childhood for a minute, you know you learned fear and, consequently, you learned to experience certain things with fear. Judgment, for example, is a word that brings up discomfort, not comfort, for most of you. Where did you learn that reaction? By contrast, if you review your childhood, you likely experienced pure happiness and curiosity about the unknown. Later, you learned to fear the unknown. It's in your truth of Self that you once again experience a pure state of curiosity—and embrace life beyond the known.

LOVE

Throughout the early chapters of this book, love is referenced in a far more profound way than, perhaps, you're accustomed to thinking about the word. I'm not just talking about the kind of love that filmmakers explore in a romantic comedy.

I've discussed the truth of Self as being love. That it's defined by all love-based emotions. That to be present means an existence dominated by love and loving experiences. That, when you're present, conscious, and/or mindful, you're not only nourishing the love, but you are in absence of fear. You're not just living your thoughts, you've moved beyond your cognition.

If all of this seems a bit esoteric, let's put the kind of love we're discussing in more relatable terms.

Most of you want to experience fulfillment and happiness in your life. If it remains elusive, it's because you're trying to get away from unhappy challenges. Or, maybe, you're looking externally for happiness. For example, many people work hard to make everyone around them happy. They believe that if they're good enough to make others happy, that they'll also find happiness. Yet, happiness remains elusive because they are trying to escape their fear of not being good enough; they're avoiding the true source of their happiness— love of Self. Love is not found in an external source or in a cognitive-behavioral world because it is a feeling within you.

You don't *do* love. You *experience* it. Because in truth, you are love!

If you are aware of feeling love or happiness in life, you certainly want to build on that feeling. For some, however, that's easier said than done. So, how do you build on a feeling of love? For starters, consciously acknowledge the positive experience you are having—and celebrate it. Often, our most joyous experiences are fleeting. Too fleeting.

For example, say you are working on a challenging problem, and you finally discover a solution. You think to yourself, "Wow! I did it!" And, then, you move on to the next project. In contrast, when you were actively struggling with that challenge, you probably were frustrated, cursing, telling everyone the story, thinking about it in bed at night, etc. You invested a lot of time and thought into the frustration of the challenge. Yet, when you succeed, there's only a moment of satisfaction before you begin focusing on the next challenge. That needs to be reversed. When you have a positive accomplishment, a happy moment, celebrate it! No matter how small it seems, make it conscious and acknowledge the good.

In this life, it's the love experiences that make you feel alive. Learn to be conscious of them—and to celebrate them—so that you're building your life on satisfying, empowering feelings. This may help you create more awareness of Self in your life. It also will help you become comfortable with inward experiences. It's in the love and acceptance of Self that we release our judgments and feel the freedom of this life. It's in the love that we are present. It's in the love that we are most comfortable in our skin and living without suffering.

FEAR

Anytime in this life that you feel a fear-based emotion, you are experiencing a challenge. All challenges are learned from experiences with Other. Therefore, they are of your past. The past, as discussed, is part of how you experience this physical existence. It's with purpose that you experience a past. The past is there for you to heal challenges and the fear-based emotions or experiences associated with them—because it's in the past where you learned the fear-based emotions from experiences imposed upon you. *There is no other reason for a past other than to heal.*

When you have anxiety about something that has yet to occur, you're projecting your past into the future. So, fear-based emotions or experiences are for no other reason but to heal and, ultimately, to unveil the truth of Self and the experience of love.

If all fear is representing the past, then it is not in the present. If you are experiencing a fear or defensive experience, you are not in the present; you're having an experience connected to your past. When you take something personally, you have reacted with the past to a symbol in the present. If that learned fear is now being projected into the future, you also are not in the present.

Truth is in the present—where there is no past connection, and the future has yet to be designed. To heal or shift from the fear is to be present.

LOVE VERSUS FEAR: CONCLUSION

In any given event or relationship in life, you can be aware of your inner experience. Is it love-based or fear-based? The more attuned you are to your Self, the sooner you'll identify and know your inner experience. As you master life, there can be times when you quickly shift back to Self and acceptance after a fear-based reaction; there also can be times when you no longer experience some fear-based emotions. Can we really evolve beyond all fear in this lifetime? I don't know, but it sure has been a joy working toward a life without fear.

When you are enjoying a loving, fun experience, embrace it, celebrate it, and wonder how to duplicate it ad infinitum. It's important to pull together the understanding of the experiences, love and fear, while also focusing on the acceptance.

To move beyond fear, you must be able to accept it, understand it—and release it. Every identification or acknowledgement of a fear, or an uncomfortable experience, is a fresh opportunity for growth. If you can surrender into that truth, you will be able to find joy as a state of existence. At that point, fearful or uncomfortable experiences become just another opportunity for growth and release of that which weighs you down.

TRUTH VERSUS ILLUSION

Love is truth. Fear is illusion. Once you understand if you are feeling fear or love, you've simultaneously clarified truth and illusion. Ultimately, if you are to experience unconditional acceptance and love, then you will see fear as creating illusions, and impediments, to your truth.

This is another avenue into understanding Self and life. As mentioned earlier, life's truths are very few—but the mastery of them takes lifetimes. So, how do you use this as an avenue to heal the challenges? Let's dig deeper.

TRUTH

As you journey into your Self and your internal experiences, you are venturing in a form of truth. You are gaining awareness of the river of feelings (the physical form of emotion). Where the Self feels limited, it is experiencing illusion and separation. Where it is feeling expansive, it is experiencing truth and unity.

Let's say, for the purposes of this teaching, that as you become aware of your inner existence and experiences, you are becoming aware of *a* truth—your truth. Let's define that truth as your conscious awareness of that which limits you with fear and illusion, as well as that which opens you up with love and truth. That awareness alone means you are focused on truth and love of Self because you can feel the limitations of fear and the freedom of love. That is "Speaking Your Truth." Truth is you in the present, aware of the influences of the past as they pertain to your present. Ultimately, truth is the Oneness. Truth is revealed in love, acceptance, and wisdom. You will know this greater truth as you gain an awareness of your language and speak the current truth within you. That language allows you to know you (love) versus that which was put upon you (fear).

ILLUSION

The illusions in this life are created by fear. Fear and its illusions have great purpose in this life, which is why Other puts it upon you. That purpose, as you have seen in the Note C parable (Chapter 1), is to help you experience and define *your* truth by creating the illusion that you are separate. Illusions are generated from past fear-based experiences—fear of separation or loneliness, fear of judgment, fear of death, fear of aggression, etc.

Let's return to the idea of Note C. When Note C is out of tune, it perceives itself as separate from the chord—but it is not. It is always a part of the chord. It just sounds "off," and so it can "hear" itself beyond the harmony of the chord. The illusion of being separate from the chord sets the stage for Note C to *fear not being a part of the chord.*

The darkness or suffering in life is illusion. It is there only to help define the light or truth of Self. It furthers says that challenges in your life are illusions to Self. To truly embrace life, you also must be willing to embrace the suffering—only to transcend it. Too often people identify with the suffering, and they leave behind life and freedom. The suffering is directly related to the challenges in this life. They are here for you to heal. On the other side of the suffering is the healing and unveiling of the Self.

On the other side of suffering is life.

> *Example 4.4.* Imagine that you are a spark inside a flame. You don't know that you're a spark because you cannot distinguish you, as a spark, from the flame. That is until, as a spark, you shoot off from the flame and into the darkness. You *appear* temporarily separate from the fire. You find yourself surrounded by darkness. *You feel alone and frightened.* You are not aware of the illusion of separation and that, in truth, you are still a part of the flame. The experience you just had is part of being a spark inside a flame; sparks jetty off periodically and then return to the flame. By perceiving separateness in that moment, you are experiencing an illusion that leads to fear. It takes the presence of the dark to illuminate the truth of you as the light. But the dark is not of you or about you. It is, simply, that which allows you to feel separate.

Often in my years of teaching, I have had people say, "So, you are going to tell me that if I am face to face with a tiger that my fear is an illusion?"

My response is: "Ultimately, yes. If you did not have a fear of death or a learned fear of the tiger, you would be in balance with and united with the tiger." The illusions of this life often are steeped in your fear of death, which is yet another illusion. There is no death, just a new beginning. What if you could conceptualize the soul and its passage to the other side without fear of death?

What would you be afraid of then?

TRUTH VERSUS ILLUSION: CONCLUSION

As you transcend the illusion of fear, you become aware of the truth of Self. You open your heart to greater acceptance and compassion for Self and people. It's in that acceptance that you know truth.

> Truth is love.
> Love is True Self.
> Love unites.
> Illusion is fear.
> Fear fragments.

When you're feeling alone or abandoned, you're seeing the illusion of separation created from the darkness of fear. When you feel acceptance and love, you are experiencing truth. Ultimately, in life, Other must be an illusion if you're to understand there is no such thing as separation. In other words, you may be Note C—but, really, you are just a critical part of the one chord.

SELF VERSUS OTHER

By becoming aware of when you are comfortable versus uncomfortable, you categorize your experience as love versus fear, respectively. This is where you begin the process of discerning your inner experience and defining what is Self and what belongs to Other. It is in the illusion of being separate that most of your fear is manifested.

As you embrace the inward search, you begin to be aware of your Self, your body, and your emotions in contrast to what you have taken on from Other. Therefore, you become aware of your joys *and* your challenges. Let's drill down on that idea.

- All joyous experiences open and expand your Self.

- Your challenges, as noted earlier, are events and experiences that leave you feeling uncomfortable because they "go against" or limit your Self. All challenges come from Other—other people, other things, other events, culture, systems, institutions, etc.

- All joyful, comfortable, or love-based emotions define and illuminate the truth and Self.

- All uncomfortable or fear-based emotions have an external limiting effect on Self and are illusions because they were learned from or originated in Other.

- All joyful or loving experiences have an internal expansive effect, unveil your wisdom, and originate within your Self.

- All fearful experiences have an external limiting effect, elicit a defense, and were put upon you by Other.

As you learn to define the experiences you wish to have, you open your Self to knowing who you are, separate from Other. You become aware of your feelings as rooted in love or fear. Subsequently, you begin to see the consequential truth or the illusion in those feelings, as they relate to your life. This leads to a life based on *what you want to experience* (Example 4.5.a) rather than what others want you to experience (Example 4.5.b).

Example 4.5.a. You and a friend agree to get together on a Friday night. You imagine the two of you going to a local hangout that you both enjoy and, hopefully, running into more of your friends. Your friend, on the other hand, is imagining a good movie and dinner. Neither of you say anything until Friday morning. Your friend calls and says, "Hey! I thought we'd go to a movie tonight! I looked up the times; we can grab dinner before it starts." Inside you feel a disappointment, but you speak your truth and say, "Well, I thought we might head over to that pub we like. Is there an earlier movie? We can catch the film and then grab a bite afterward. I bet some of our friends will be there."

Example 4.5.b. You and a friend agree to get together on a Friday night. You're not sure what you're in the mood to do, so you don't have a suggestion. On Friday morning, your friend calls and says, "Hey! I thought we'd go to a movie tonight! I looked up the times; we can grab dinner before it starts." You agree to the plan, but you don't feel excited—and you don't really know why. Still, you don't want to disappoint your friend by going against the idea.

As you can see from the above examples, knowing what you wish to experience is the cornerstone of learning to express your true Self. By doing that, you avoid getting caught in a web of reacting and following—because you're either reacting to the expectations or needs of Other, or you're following Other simply to please, comfort or appease them. This reaction/response is almost always out of a need to be good enough which, as we've discussed, is steeped in your *fear of not being good enough*. Fears in life were developed by external experiences put upon you by Other. They're part of the past.

Let's look at how you can identify your experience of Self by gaining an awareness of where you are experiencing Other—and then separating the two.

THE INFLUENCE OF OTHER IN EARLY CHILDHOOD: HOW CHALLENGES ARE BORN

You came into this physical life with an initial experience of separation and fear, and yet you were very connected to your energetic self. That combination of influences to your perception of life made your perceptions as a child unique to others around you.

In Figure 12, the circle around you also is *of you*. It has two meanings—one physical, one energetic. For now, let's focus on the physical meaning.

Physically, the circle represents your physical world separate from everyone on the outside of the circle. It represents your unique perception of the world different from the perspective of all others on the outside of the circle. It symbolizes your experience as defined by your unique perceptions. The circle also speaks to the limitations of the physical perceptions that shape your view of life.

Your early life experiences shaped your life and its purpose. Shortly after you were born, you were taught how to think, feel, and be, as defined by those around you (Figure 13). Your parents, fearing that they couldn't soothe you, would say, "Stop crying," or "Shhhh." In trying to prevent you from falling, they might grab you or hold you tight while saying, "No!" But in trying to keep you safe, your parents are forging your fears out of their own fears of not being good enough parents. Because what kind of parent can't protect their child? It's just one example of how, in your early years, your parents are your most influential teachers. This is by design.

Later in your childhood, you had siblings, grandparents and maybe extended family who also told you what to think, what to believe, and how to behave. Before long, your friends were influencing how you dressed, or telling you what to like and who to like. Teachers taught you what to know, how to learn, what grades you needed to make, and how good you were or were not. Then there was community, religion, society, systems. All of these different external influences, using their respective devices, placed their teachings upon you through expectations and rules. In essence, from your earliest weeks of life, you were inundated by beliefs, opinions, and fears generated by Other.

Figure 14 depicts you surrounded by these external influences. Each figure represents a person, experience, entity, institution, or system.

The people, groups, cultures, events, structures (and more) represented by this illustration comprise Other. All of the rules, expectations, fears, etc., from Other, hid or buried the Soulful Self (*who* you are). In those moments, as mentioned earlier, Other is like dark, stormy clouds that hide the beauty of bright sunlight.

The Soulful Self is the part of you that, when present in all relationships and aspects of your life, guides you to living in a state of joy, freedom, and abundance. It opens through a spontaneous expression of Self. It is the impact of Other that can keep the Soulful Self hidden and or limited. When Other offers unconditional love and acceptance, the Soulful

Self is identified and expanded. When Other appears like dark clouds, it creates the illusion that the sun is gone.

Your Soulful Self is the sun that is always a bright light on the other side of those clouds. In this life, your free will decides which clouds you wish to part—and how much of your light you wish to show.

SELFOTHER LANGUAGE

As mentioned earlier, The Sage's Template™ uses language (both spoken and imagined) to open the doors to healing the Self. Language is critical in this physical life, especially if you wish to unveil the freedom of a conscious life while living within society.

Communication is the basis of every relationship—and language is one form of communicating. You are being shown a potential way to know your True Self beyond Other by separating Self and Other through a conscious awareness and understanding of language. I will use language and physical experience to help you begin separating your Self from Other.

As a child, you were taught by Other what is acceptable according to Other's needs. As a result, it was critical that, as a child, you were able to perceive what Other preferred and expected. You feared that if you weren't good enough to meet those expectations you would be abandoned. You knew as a child that, if you were abandoned, you would not survive. Consequently, you learned that the needs and expectations of all Other were of the utmost importance to your survival. In other words, you learned that Other's expectations and needs were "more valuable" than your needs, interests and expressions.

Your language grew as a result of this learning. You speak mostly from what (and how) you learned from all the influences that comprise Other. Reflect back to Figure 7 on page 17; this is how you began your SelfOther language. You also learned to speak from (and respond to) expectations or assumptions. You may "read" the person across from you and, from your assumptions of them, integrate their expectations into your language, response or reaction. You also may integrate your perception of them into how you relate to them. You may talk with another person about your ideas, beliefs, or thoughts—only to realize later that they were learned and not completely of you. This is why it's called SelfOther language.

The goal is to speak from your Self and of your Self. Too often, especially in your early and formative years, you are speaking from what you have learned, not from your *truth*. You may be speaking to gain approval, but that is not your truth. You may speak of your religion, but it is the religion you were taught to believe. You may speak of your political affiliation, but those political views were presented to you. You may even choose a career because you were told you'd excel in that field. All of these forms of communication of Self are really SelfOther forms.

In these upcoming sections, language and accessible examples will be used to illustrate the differences between Self and what is learned from Other.

SELF

Listening to your words and your breath set you on a path to unveiling your true Self. Only some of your thoughts have words associated with them; of those thoughts with words attached, only some are heard and/or spoken. That tells you that there are a lot of choices being made within you before you even begin to interact with Other. That's why it's so important to *listen to your Self.*

Growing up, Other did not listen to or explore you. They did not ask you who you were and what you were all about. For example, when you were young, adults may have asked what you wanted to be when you grew up. If you responded, the adults probably smiled and said something like, "Isn't that cute." But did any of them ask a follow-up question? Like, why? Or what's the source of that dream? They were amused—but not enough to explore an interest *in you*. They were too busy assuming they knew what you needed and who you were—and then telling you how to meet *their* expectations.

It's likely that you experienced a sense of not being known, of not being heard, because you weren't given the opportunity to introduce your Self to Other. Feelings of being unheard were buried under your need to be good enough just to be acknowledged. It's an experience like this, and the feelings attached to it, that leads you to assume—and try to meet—the expectations of Other. It's also how you learned not to focus on the knowing of Self.

> *Example 4.6.* A mother came to see me and brought her 3-year-old son. He was playing with a couple of toy trucks; he'd roll one of the trucks up the wall and then back to the floor. Clearly, he was having a great adventure in

his imagination regarding the trucks and their travels. The mother, however, was not having it. She kept telling him to keep the truck on the floor, that it didn't belong on the wall. At first, I told her I was very OK with it, but she explained that she wanted her son to learn good manners. It didn't occur to her to ask her son why the truck was going up and down the wall. In that moment, the boy's imagination and creativity became stifled. He was left unknown and unheard by the mom. He could have learned those boundaries in subsequent years, but, at age 3, he needed to be encouraged to dream and imagine.

You were raised to be obedient (at some level) to all Other. This made you focus on the people and institutions or events that were in your life. You had an external focus. You bought into the beliefs *they* had about you. Self was left behind in that focus. As noted earlier, you still know your Self—it's just hidden behind all the expectations and assumptions.

The beliefs instilled in you came from assumptions, judgments, and expectations put upon you by Other. You bought into those beliefs—because there was no known way to be heard or to explore who you really are.

> ***Example 4.7***. Peyton has a high IQ, but he has anxiety and difficulty participating in a large classroom. Consequently, Peyton does not perform well at school. The school system, and his friends and parents, all assume that Peyton isn't smart. And Peyton is treated as if that's the case. Peyton understands the work, but fear prevents him from thriving in a traditional classroom setting. One day, at age 13, someone tells Peyton that he's not capable of succeeding and will not amount to anything. Peyton finally gives in to the judgment—and gives up on any intellectual pursuits. Today, Peyton is aware of an attention deficit, and he even understands that he has an above-average IQ. Still, he defines himself as "not able."

Your true, or Soulful, Self exists behind the presenting self, which is colored by the Other pocket. Externally, you present a self that bought into the definitions and beliefs put upon you by Other. You were not conscious of your Self; the person you came to know developed from the judgments and assumptions of Other. These old beliefs limit you and your freedom.

Fortunately, there's so much more to this story. As you master your challenges, you unveil your truth and Soulful Self, as well as the freedom that accompanies it.

OTHER

You entered this life with Other surrounding you and communicating to you (Figure 13). You understood that communication in your own unique way. Furthermore, because of the vast difference in the way you were experiencing the world versus the way Other was experiencing you, you were not known or understood completely by Other. In your curiosity, you were taking in the information of Other to make sense of your experience. It's how Other begins to have such a profound influence over you.

Other is comprised, in part, of institutions within your culture and society. Those institutions are a constant in their rule structure. They influence (and are influenced by) society and culture. Your family and friends are of these institutions, society and culture. Based on your experiences and the people in your life, Other can represent countless influences. Imagine all the potential fears and teachings to which that translates. Fears and teachings that you absorb.

Despite all this, there remains a conflict inside—you versus Other—as you try to be yourself during your younger years. Unfortunately, it's not easy to find your True Self as a youth, or even into your teens and early 20s given the influence of Other. By the design of life, your parents are a key source of many of your challenges, even if they were not there. I've had patients who've pointed to something that happened in school as the most influential impact on their life. Yet, once they begin to unravel the experience, they see that they coped with (and assimilated) the school episode because of challenges already in place from previous experiences—many from their parents and family environment.

> *Example 4.8.* A middle school girl is getting teased because she has an unusual looking ear. She becomes sad and depressed; she feels like no one will like her because she is ugly. She acquiesces to the judgment and loses her self-esteem.

> The question is, what teachings were in place prior to that incident that set the stage for her to take the judgments so personally? If she had confidence going into middle school, she would have handled the situation differently. The teaching could be as vague as one of the parents, worried their daughter

would be teased, unintentionally drew unnecessary attention to the oddness of her ear from an early age. Perhaps, she was teased at home by a sibling—and the parents didn't stop it. Maybe, her parent(s) tried to give her hairstyles that covered the ear. It also could have been that she grew up in a home where she was constantly in trouble for not doing things "right," and so her confidence already was low as she struggled to be good enough. There are myriad possibilities. Whatever the answer (or answers), the experiences were absorbed by the little girl in a way that depleted her self-esteem prior to being teased in middle school.

What if, instead, the teachings at home were empowering? What if she were aware not only of her ear but also of her great attributes? What if she had learned to be assertive and to believe in herself? Perhaps then, when the teasing began, she would have possessed the tools to tell the children they were mean and that, if they were going to act like that, she didn't want anything to do with them. The incident still would've hurt, but it wouldn't have been so debilitating.

As the above example illustrates, your parents are the most influential Other—for a variety of reasons. They're not the sole influence, and they're certainly not to blame for all of your challenges. Still, your parents are in your life with great purpose.

So, what else comprises Other? Think beyond the obvious and consider any Other—a teacher, a TV show, a friend, a club or organization, a comic book—that may have had an influence in your development. Don't dwell on the answer, just allow yourself to see the vastness of Other so that you can understand that the simplicity in life will be found inside you rather than looking to the external.

Your physical experience of this life is constructed of challenges and gifts. The challenges were learned and incongruent with Self and, therefore, limiting. The gifts were (and are) those experiences that were congruent with Self and helped you to feel expansive.

In the Note C parable (Chapter 1), you learned that challenges relate to being out of tune. Yet, you understand what Self (Note C) "sounds and feels" like as you become aware of the healing (tuning) process. As you become "in tune," you have awareness of what and who you are as you align with the sound of the chord. You know your presence! Now, when you are a part of the One, you are aware of your integral presence with the One—your sound amid the chord.

Other is always external to Self. It may be assimilated within your physical experience but the source of fear or incongruence is from an external source. That is why I had you look at the numerous external sources. You grew up learning to look to the external for reinforcement, love, guidance, and more. So, your focus is likely external most of the time.

This is why, for example, you may find yourself admiring another individual. The very characteristics you are admiring in them, however, are characteristics of you. You're just not conscious of them—because it wasn't reinforced by Other.

Hopefully, you're starting to see the complexities of misdirection and misunderstanding that have been imparted from the beginning by Other. Whether these were intentional or unintentional is neither here nor there. You experienced all of this inside you. Therefore, it's inside you where you experienced the judgment, expectations, and assumptions from Other. Thus, it's inside you where the separation of Self from Other must begin.

It's also inside you where you can start to simplify these external challenges and, ultimately, master them.

Expectations always come from Other. Expectations always are external to your Self. They block you from life and freedom. They block you from your dreams. They create suffering. You don't put expectations upon your Self; you set goals. You learned expectations. It's from this learning that you assimilated and accommodated the words of Other into your own patterns.

CONCLUSION

Other plays a key role in this life. It sets the stage for your purpose on this plane to be experienced. You came into this life to have an experience. That experience includes the fear that you will either suffer or master (completely or partially, given your free will).

It is through teachings by Other that you develop a sense of fear without awareness of its illusion. Your true Self, once separate from Other, begins to come into focus through mastery of the challenges that influenced the illusion of a presenting self. It is the Self that can differentiate the truth and love separate from the illusions and fear. It is the Self that will teach Other who and what you are.

Your language can continuously reflect the truth of Self once you begin understanding your Self and its experiences in absence of the illusions created by (and a part of) Other. This is why it's critical to become aware of your emotions and your Self.

As you become aware of your truth and emotions, you are beginning to split Self from Other. As you begin to understand the difference between Self (comfortable feeling) and Other (uncomfortable feeling), you can identify language that's coming from the Other pocket or the Self pocket. Your language eventually can be spontaneously spoken from that awareness. Furthermore, your Self wishes to experience being known and heard by Other. As you gain an awareness of your own experiences, separate from Other, you will want to teach Other who and what you are, in truth.

Conclusion of Physical Experience

So far, you have seen the use of the Template for the physical aspect of life. In your physical life, you can address your challenges, unveil your truth, and define your Self to Other. It's a simple way to recognize when you are standing in alignment with your Self, as opposed to when you are off balance from the incongruent learnings from Other. You now have seen how this part of the Template can be a guide as far as developing your dreams, as well as your purpose in this life. This part of the Template helps you focus on and define the experiences that YOU wish to have.

In the physical experience of life, you experience duality. You learn through this duality. The Template simplifies the duality to Self versus Other, Truth versus Illusion, and Love versus Fear. It uses the duality for you to set your Self and Truth apart from the Fear and Illusion; this way, you can become aware of the unity and oneness of life beyond the physical life as you perceive it to be.

All of your experiences in this life have and will have a physical component. It's inside you that you experience all that was put upon you and all that you learned (knowledge and ego). It's also inside you that you know your truth and the truth of life (knowingness and wisdom). The physical aspect of life offers you the opportunity to tease these two inner aspects apart by separating the fear (ego) from the truth (wisdom). It offers you the opportunity to separate the outer (stage set from Chapter 1) from the inner (your experience).

It's the physical life that is the storyline of your play of life. You are here, as a soul, to have a physical experience. Much like the fear that defines this physical experience, your soul is ultimately using free will to transcend the physical and "know" its existence in the infinite energetic realm. The spiritual or energetic realm of the Soul and its journey in this life is a critical aspect of the Template.

Next, let's focus on the soulfulness or energy of this life and your experiences: the spiritual journey.

CHAPTER

5

Self—The Energetic Experience

INTRODUCTION

The pieces of our puzzle are starting to come together. You now understand that the physical life is driven by your energetic, or soulful, aspect. As you learn to look inward— healing challenges and uncovering wisdom along the way—you're able to see this life with greater clarity. That's because the physical aspect is defined by the inner truth of what you know about life. Remember, this life is your soul having an experience.

A critical piece of your mastery of this life involves unveiling your Self. One way to do that is to separate Self from Other, starting with both internal dialogue and spoken language. Ultimately, the purpose of mastery is to unleash the Soulful Self.

Let's stay with the idea of using language for a conscious journey to enlightenment. If the soul is energy, and emotion is energy, you will use emotion as the language of your Soul. The Soul energy has its own language—emotions and intuition.

Emotions can be divided into love-based and fear-based emotions. All humans have the same emotions but feel them as unique responses to life. Emotions are felt based on different stimuli or experiences, but the language is the same for all humans. It's the emotional language that bridges the Soul to the physical body and its life. It's the *energy of the emotion* that converts to *feelings in the body*. And it's through emotions that intuition is felt or read.

SOULFUL DEVELOPMENT IN VERY EARLY CHILDHOOD

You are an energetic being as well as a physical being. There is a life energy that also makes you unique and gives life to this human form. Energy is a constant. Energy always has been, always is, and always will be. It may change form, but it always continues and cannot be destroyed.

Most will agree that they have a life energy that embodies their physical self in this life. This is commonly referred to as the Soul. Your Soul is believed to enter this life at conception and leave this life upon death. The Soul is *the truth of who you are* as a human being. This is why you hear people say you are a Soul having a human experience.

When you were born, you had an awareness of this soulful existence that began at conception, but you quickly forgot it. Your first years of life were dominated by your intuition because your intellect had yet to actively define the surrounding world. You could sense and "know" the experience of your parents and the world around you. If you were in a safe environment, you could "feel" that. If the environment was unsafe, you sensed that as well. This intuitiveness is more highly developed in early childhood than even adults tend to realize.

In that sense, early childhood was a more soulful, pure existence. You were quite intuitive and aware of what was happening around you and within you. Slowly, as your intellect developed and society shaped your thoughts and behaviors, you may have lost conscious awareness of (and connection with) your intuition.

But your perception of life was completely unique from anyone else outside the circle of your perceptions. And you are built upon these experiences.

THE EARLY PRESENCE OF TRUE SELF

As previously stated, you came into this physical life with an initial experience of separation and fear—and yet you were very connected to your energetic self. That combination of influences made your perceptions as a child unique to others around you. Look at Figure 15. The circle represents both your *physical* and *energetic* world.

The energetic meaning of the circle is that when you first enter this experience of life you are connected to your energy world through intuition and emotion. Energetically, the circle is a representation of that life-energy (or Soul) because the circle has no beginning or end. And energy has no beginning or end. It always is. It may change forms, but the energy is constant. To further this point, when twisted, the circle becomes the sign for infinity. Therefore, the circle around your wee self represents the connection you had and have to the infinite (from where you came) and to your Soul. It is the infinite from which your Soul came that sources your intuition, emotion, and wisdom. The circle represents the connection to the energy aspect of your being as well as the unique way in which you will approach this life.

As part of the circle, you are all that you came into this life to be. You are aware of your journey and its experience. You are aware of that "place" from which you came. You are aware of the uninfluenced truth of You. With your connection to that circle, you are perceiving all experiences around you with great intuition and senses. You are truly having a unique experience of life from anyone outside your circle.

If you put both the physical and energetic being together, it forms your Soulful Self. It is that aspect of life that embodies you in your pure light form and houses the information regarding your purpose on this plane for this lifetime. Upon birth you have an awareness of both the physical and energetic aspects of your existence. Figure 15 represents your True Self or Soulful Self upon birth.

The Soul's Language

As previously mentioned, the Soul's language is a constant because energy is a constant. Your Soul is connected to your higher self, which constantly communicates with emotion. The Soul is in a constant state of manifesting. Initially, in this life, you may not be conscious of what you are manifesting and what you are doing to manifest. This may be because your emotions are at the core of your intentions and, in this physical life, you were seduced away from your inner knowing to focus on the knowledge from Other. To know your emotional flow is to tap into the energy of your being.

Ultimately, the Soul is united and is one with all that is. That *One* is of energy—love energy. So, where you may experience fear-based emotions, the Soul is telling you that you are limited, trapped or held back. Once you are aware of that language, it becomes simple to identify when you are limited (having fear-based emotions) and when you are expansive (having love-based emotions). The limited experience was put upon you by Other, and the expansive is your truth unveiling your Soulful Self. You can choose to move beyond those limiting experiences and shift into your Soulful Self.

Free will says you always have choice. There is free will soulfully and physically. Remember the "Life's a Stage" parable in Chapter 1? Recall how you chose this life and its secondary characters—but you left free will for all the characters in the play by allowing them to improvise. It's through free will that you choose to suffer or to heal. Soulfully, you are aware of why you are here and what your main experience is to be. You are aware of what healing can occur in this experience or another—and yet free will continues to exist in your choices regarding how, when, and if. Ultimately, free will is about the overall experience of the Soul and its presence.

Soulfully, you may have had experiences elsewhere (also known as past lives)[6] that ended without your Soul healing some of the challenges. Those challenges could have carried into this experience for healing. Therefore, in this lifetime or experience, you will have occurrences that resurrect those "past" experiences that are looking to heal. Everything you need for healing, therefore, is in this life. It is your Soul's free will that accesses the healing. It's your physical Self that plays out the healing—or not. Your Soul is experiencing this life, and this life, in general, is about fears and the healing that results from understanding and overcoming them.

Ultimately, thoughts create. Thoughts are energy. However, in this physical life you learn to use thoughts for knowledge. That means they can be anchored in the fears, limitations, and logic of this realm and learning. Your thoughts, therefore, often are based in ego in your physical life. In your spiritual existence, when intention and thought are unified and aligned, you manifest. The spirit realm "hears" your inner voice and your intention. Whatever is in alignment within you will be manifested due to your free will. That is true for fear or love. This is the truth of why you have thoughts.

> *Example 5.1*.[7] In high school, a young man loves his high school sweetheart so much that he prays to God to make the young woman his forever. Eventually they break up and he moves on to marry another woman. Later in their married life, he and his wife run into the high-school sweetheart. In talking with his high-school sweetheart, he realizes that they have nothing in common and that the true love of his life is his current wife. Some would say, "Thank God for unanswered prayers," but there are no unanswered prayers. His verbal prayers in high school were for a great love like what he was experiencing. His prayer to "make her his forever" included his fear of losing her. Therefore, the prayer had two parts: the conscious component for love, like the kind he was experiencing at the time; and the intention or hidden component of fear over possibly losing her. Both parts were granted: the fear of loss and the great love!

---

[6]   The Soul does not know time or space, so the concept of past does not exist. In this life, however, we perceive of a past for our healing. Because of our perception of time, we are only able to be aware of what we have already experienced. To us, the future is yet to be designed. Consequently, we say past lives because it is in our "memory" and, therefore, appears to be in our past. To the soul, it is an experience elsewhere.

[7]   This is paraphrased from Garth Brooks (1990), "Unanswered Prayers," Capital Nashville.

The soul's language is very powerful. It can be love-based or fear-based. If fear-based, it may be part of your background thoughts and old beliefs that you think you can ignore. But, in reality, those thoughts and beliefs are fueling and/or sabotaging your experiences in this life. You may find your Self wishing for a greater love, better health, or financial freedom. And yet these desires seem elusive. That's because of the soulful intention. Remember, you are here to heal the challenges that are blocking you from the flow of abundance. Soulfully, you are aware of the challenges of this life. It's your choice to unveil that which limits you—and to heal it. Through healing, you open your Self to the soulfulness of this existence—beyond the fear. Trusting life. Surrendering to it.

ENERGETIC DIMENSION OF THE SOUL

The Soul comes from a place of love and abundance. Upon shedding the body, the Soul experiences that love—and there is no ebbing the flow of abundance. Abundance is pure freedom. That is the energetic essence of pure love, defined by humans. Energetically, there is only abundance. Physically, it's your fears that create the illusion of being outside the flow of abundance and freedom.

It's in the energetic dimensions beyond this three-dimensional existence that duality vanishes and separation between "You and Me" disappears. As you become conscious of the expansiveness of existence, you feel love, freedom, abundance, and infinity. To put it another way: When you are living in a state of love and acceptance, you feel the expansiveness of existence. Words, however, don't do justice to what lies beyond.

It is the intuition that is pure connection to the energetic oneness. Yet, as intuition is interpreted in this physical realm, language and perception limit its messaging. It is through the energetic expansiveness that you can open to the realm beyond this duality. Duality promotes separateness. You can become aware of the oneness. You can become aware there is no separation and no duality. Ultimately, you can transcend this experience of separate and see only one. It is the energetic or Soulful Self that opens you to that possibility.

> *Exercise 5.2*. In meditation, listen to crystal bowls or high-frequency music. Once in a focused, relaxed state, follow one note as it hums into a blend with the whole. Continue to focus on that experience until you are the original

sound—until you feel your Self melding with the overall sound. Infinite sound can be felt.

In this life, one place (of several) that you can consciously experience the oneness of pure love is through lovemaking. If all gates are open within each of you, the expansiveness may blend. During that level of intimate expression, you can experience a complete absence of the separate bodies and unite in oneness—while, at the same time, feeling your own presence and your partner's presence. That experience is a taste of the pure essence of existence.

CONCLUSION

As you embrace the soulfulness of your existence, you grow beyond the limitations of the physical and into abundance. When you meditate, you can cross the rainbow bridge to the energetic world and begin to feel the oneness.

Emotions are the language of the soul—the same set of emotions shared by all. It's a language that reveals the unity of all. Consciously, then, you can transcend the duality of this life and experience that unity by reading your emotional language and following your intuition.

It's critical to life mastery that you embrace challenges. It's through the transcendence of fear-based emotions and experiences that you define the essence of you. You may want to believe that if you stay in meditation that you can stay in a state of love, but actually that thought carries the fear of doubt. It's a subtle avoidance of living life and transcending the fears. If you wish to live in a state of love, you must be willing to suffer the pain that comes with confronting challenges.

Your energy self is always connected to your physical self. You are just unconscious of the relationship. By gaining an awareness of the energy of your emotion, you can alter and influence your dreams. That's why being conscious of the experience is a bridge between physical and energetic life experiences. It opens you to true freedom as you slowly allow Self to be tethered to the physical realm while experiencing it as the egoless observer of the Soulful Self. As the observer, you will see why certain challenges appear and how they allow you to further transcend this duality.

6

Using The Sage's Template™ to Master Your Life

INTRODUCTION

Life is a journey that occurs within you—and is from you. Therefore, the mastery of life occurs as your current inner experience evolves into the experience *you wish to have*.

However, as we've already discovered, you learned to interact with life through an external focus of what Other wants. In essence, that focus keeps you from you. The only way to have awareness of the experience you're having, let alone the one you wish to have, is to separate Self from Other. For others to know who you really are—and for you to fulfill your dreams and desires—you must learn to speak your truth.

The basis of all life is experience. This is your life, so it's about your experience. Most of you wish to have an experience that involves love and acceptance, freedom and compassion. But it's not easy to find such joy when you're out of tune with Self and the experience of you. Too often, you're listening to the needs, expectations or demands of Other. Thus, as you search for happiness, you're looking externally through the definitions of Others.

This experience of happiness never will be yours because it's "theirs." When you're trying so hard to meet someone else's definition of life, love, and adventure, you lose sight of your Self. You may try your entire life to "find" love, but you're not going to find a fulfilling love when you're following someone else's lead. What you wish for in this life must come from inside YOU.

Understanding your experience in such a profound way can shape the interactions that you have with Other. For example, you may be aware of feeling insecure (your experience) in a particular relationship, and you clearly state that to Other. Now, Other can feel compassion for your position, and together you can move through the insecurity. You're able to achieve greater freedom and intimacy in the relationship because you've opened your Self (and your heart) to the other person in this relationship.

Another example: Let's say you don't enjoy the experience of school. However, your family, your culture, your religion, and perhaps other influences, have pushed you to attend college. Even though all your friends and siblings are going to college, your desire is to either join the Peace Corps or open a maintenance business. If you do what Other demands, you'll likely suffer through college until you quit, fail, or begrudgingly graduate. If you are clear and confident within your Self that you do not want to attend college, you can voice those convictions and follow your own dreams, regardless of the opinions or judgments of Other. In the end, you find great fulfillment by following your own path.

It sounds simple, but it takes an unyielding desire to focus on your Self and to diligently be mindful, or at least conscious, of your internal experience. In other words, you *must know your Self* in order to understand the experience you are having—and the experience you wish to have.

The irony of doing such an internal deep dive—of knowing your Self so well that you understand your Truth or Soulful Self—is that you gain big-picture clarity. You see connections to the greater whole. That is life mastery. It's the ultimate experience. It's being aware of challenges until they have opened you to truth. It's in that place that love and acceptance define your Self experience.

In this chapter, you will begin the journey toward life mastery by learning to use The Sage's Template™. Through the Template, you'll explore your Self so that you can be aware of the experience you're having—and aware of the experience you wish to have. You'll also begin to speak your truth, the language that teaches others about the experiences of which you're comprised.

A Review of The Sage's Template™

As you look at The Sage's Template™ (TST) (Figure 11, page 17), you see there are two general sides. On the right is a picture of you today; on the left there are two columns. Let's review the structure and definition of TST.

The illustration of you on the right shows two inner pockets. The larger one is all that was put upon you by Other (people, experiences, systems, etc.); this contains your fear and illusions of that fear. The smaller pocket is your Soulful Self, defined by the energy of love from where you came and the truth of all that you are. In short, fear is always illusion, and love is always truth.

Your spoken language is a "SelfOther" language: You think it's emanating from you, but it's typically coming from Other. It is language based on everything you learned early in life (from people, systems, culture, societal rules, etc.). That same language exists in your thoughts, which makes sense given that's where your spoken word is formed. Though it feels like you're speaking your truth, you're not. At least not yet. SelfOther language is filled with learnings from Other, the external community or world.

The left side of TST consists of two columns. The tops of those columns separate your physical life into a dualistic model of Self versus Other, Truth versus Illusion, and Love versus Fear. Because you learned to focus on the external world (Other), and its rules and expectations, the focus separated you from your Self. (This concept of separation is at the core of our life experience.) This separation sets the stage for the dualistic model from which we learn in this life.

Below the dualistic model of the physical life is the Soul and its language of Emotion. Soul is energy, and emotion is energy (until it is turned into a physical feeling). Energy is a constant, thus emotional energy is a constant, but it's not something you "feel." Fear-based energy is what creates the illusion of Soul being separated from its whole; love-based energy is where Soul feels connected to the whole. In other words, fear-based energy is when Soul feels limited and trapped; love-based energy is when Soul feels free and expansive. Emotional energy, as noted in the chart, can be divided into love-based and fear-based emotions. Physical meaning is then given to those emotions so that we can bridge the physical and energetic existence of your Soulful (or True) Self.

Know Your Self and Your Experience

This model of mastery is going to use language to help you attain goals and freedom. Language is sound with meaning; energy to which is given definition. In other words, language is sound that is energy and a constant; it has meaning to you that is love-based or fear-based. Your language is going to be the bridge between the energy experience and the physical experience of your life.

To begin the process of exploring Self, listen to your SelfOther language—including your thoughts, the gateway to your truth. Don't change your words or thoughts, just listen to them. The words of your thoughts or voice will take you into the emotion; this will help discern if you are coming from a place of truth (love) or from the illusion (fear) that "separates" you from your true or Soulful Self. Your SelfOther language may contain judgments or understandings, anger or compassion, assumptions or questions, expectations or guidance. Don't be afraid of the words or where they lead; they're serving a purpose.

Two things happen when you begin to listen to your Self. One, you are being heard by the most important person in your life—you. Two, you're beginning an inward focus. This is where life begins to be about you! It's where you start to unveil your Soulful Self by exploring the origin of your thoughts/words.

Once you get used to listening to your Self and observing your speech/thoughts, you can move to the left side of TST. In reviewing your language, capture the statement or fear or concept. Then, go to the love-based and fear-based emotions—and ask yourself where these thoughts fall. In other words, are your thoughts saying you are suffering? Or you are joyous?

If you're not sure of the exact feelings, ask yourself if the thoughts are comfortable or uncomfortable. If they are comfortable, they're on the love-based side; if they are uncomfortable, they're on the fear-based side. Be sure you are discerning comfort from familiar. You may be feeling something that is very familiar but is not comfortable.

Once you know from which side your thoughts are derived, start working your way up the column. If your thoughts are from the love-based side, you can see that they are of your truth in the physical experience of Self. Therefore, your Soulful Self is present—and you are present. You can feel a sense of expansiveness and freedom. Compassion and acceptance are present for Self and Other. When you experience this, please be sure to celebrate!

If your thoughts are fear-driven, they are fostering illusions that were put upon you by Other. Therefore, your true Soulful Self is not present—and you are not living in the moment. All fear-based emotions and thoughts, whether they're about you or someone else, engender suffering and are from the past. The thoughts and feelings are within you and are affecting your belief in yourself. They're steering you away from your truth and into the external world of Other.

By becoming aware of your thoughts and the underlying emotions that drive them, you are beginning to separate out what is You and what is Other. As you begin to define Self, an absence of separation occurs inside you. Furthermore, feelings of love grow for your Self. It is from these inner experiences that you find the experience of unity and oneness, acceptance and compassion. The irony of this life is that we must "separate" our Self from the external Other to find the absence of separation.

At this point, you are inside your world. You can identify if you're within your truth or following an illusion. So, now what?

To find freedom in this life, it's necessary to move from the right column, the Other pocket, to the left column, the Soulful Self pocket. To feel balanced or centered, your experiences must be in the left column. It is the right column or Other that throws you off balance. But here's the good news: By recognizing that fear, you're able to understand the truth of what you are.

It's not about ignoring or fighting the Other column. It's about accepting and embracing those experiences as you choose to live beyond them in a state of joy. The existence of the dark or of fear isn't going anywhere. It's up to you to grow beyond the experience of it. Once you're aware of fear-based or uncomfortable emotion or thought, it's an opportunity to shift. Most of you will not be so detailed in your efforts. You'll begin by noticing larger experiences or events that upset you in some way.

So, let's take the next step in this journey.

SEPARATING SELF FROM OTHER

You can now see that in truth you are made of love—thus, love-based feelings or experiences define you in truth. You've also learned the critical value of Other, and the fear-based experiences and feelings that they develop. Think back on the Note C parable in Chapter 1.

As you have an experience that evokes fear-based emotion or feeling, you now know that's caused by past teachings from Other that developed those emotions. You are here to move through or transcend those fears into love. Free will says that you'll decide which and how many fears you will heal. Each of you has the capacity to heal all that you choose. The more challenges you move through, the greater your freedom in this life.

Begin by identifying the fear-based emotions that are defining the experience. Use Appendix A if you need assistance. Write down all the emotions connected to the experience. Next, think about when you've felt this same way (or in a similar way) in the past. Acknowledge that experience fully and, looking at the emotions you already wrote down, see which ones you felt in the prior experience. Then ask if you felt that way prior to *that* experience. If so, acknowledge that experience and explore it. Again, review the original list of identified emotions and write down which ones you felt in this experience. And so on. Continue inching your way back through memories and acknowledging the emotions that you felt until you hit the earliest memory. Write that memory down in detail, as much as you can remember.

You are now at the place where you can begin to separate you as Self from Other. That original (or earliest remembered) memory is where you may be able to shift your fears. In the memory you have defined, ask yourself what you were experiencing prior to Other creating such fear-based emotions in you.

> ***Example 6.1.*** The memory is of you at age 5. You were playing in the sandbox. You were in the final stages of building this great castle when, out of nowhere, your parent briskly slid open the screen door and yelled at you to get in the house. Prior to that, you were feeling joy and excitement at your creation. You were inside your Self, creating and playing. You were free and carefree. In addition to the shock of the door opening so quickly, you felt fear because of the yelling. Worse yet, you were yelled at for not

responding the first time your parent asked you to come in. You honestly never heard your parent. Still, you feel like you did something wrong. You don't understand why you now feel so unsettled when, just seconds earlier, you were having the best time. The lack of congruence is disturbing, but you take it personally and leave your sandcastle behind to go inside and be obedient. You are now feeling "bad" in some way. Before your parent's arrival, however, you were feeling "good."

You now want to go back to the good feelings. Understand your Self. Show compassion for your Self. Feel the freedom from your parent's expression, which had nothing to do with you. That was coming from your mom or dad. It was all about them. Separate your Self from Other (parent). Love who you are as that child playing freely. Bask in the experience. Feel the good of who you are. Release the fear that you felt, fear put upon you by Other. Release the negative, personalized aspect of that experience. You did nothing wrong.

Once you feel the greatness of you, look at the parent through the eyes of your own beauty. See them as if they are on the other side of a two-way mirror. Imagine what was going on inside your parent that made them have the experience that they were having. Remember, it has NOTHING to do with you. It has only to do with Mom or Dad. Create a story for them that makes sense to you without you being in the story.

> **Example 6.2.** Your parent was having a rough day and was exhausted. Then s/he realized s/he forgot to finish a bit of work that needed to be completed that night. S/he wanted to get you fed, and when you didn't respond immediately s/he exploded. After feeding you, s/he was able to see the error—but s/he never shared that experience, nor did s/he ever apologize for the incident.

You can see how this story is very separate from yours. You took it personally at age 5 because you had no choice, you knew no other way. You merged Self and Other because that is what you do as a child. You are built upon those old memories. You can see from working your way back to this memory that it continues to show up in the present by staying alive in feelings about yourself and in your perceptions. Notice that we went back to *one* memory. We are not reliving your past!

Regarding your original memory, ask yourself: "What is the experience I wish to have had?" Be very clear. Write it down. Feel the love-based feelings for who you are in truth. Grow those feelings. Where do you need to feel that love in your life today? You are now beginning to create your life as you wish it to be!

You can use the above exercise for any fear-based experience in which you don't understand certain feelings you're having. It can become a very quick awareness that allows a shift. There will be a time when you do not need to go into your past so literally to define the origins of a fear. There also will be a time where the origin is no longer needed, and you just shift from that emotion to your truth by speaking your truth.

Still, it's critical that you're willing to look at past pain and its origins in the name of healing. Avoidance will keep the healing at bay. Without healing, you cannot truly live in the present.

IDENTIFYING YOUR SOULFUL SELF

In the above discussion, you learned to separate yourself from the original experience. The original experience obviously was not what you wished, but it was "put upon" you in this life with purpose. Allow yourself to remember your own history, no matter how simple or complex. In that memory, you experienced separation from love when you felt bad. You felt fear—fear over being yelled at, fear that you did something wrong, that you weren't good enough. Yet, when you pulled away from the fear and defined your own experience, separate from your parent's experience, you were able to feel compassion—and, therefore, unity with or connection to the very parent who created the original fear.

It's an example of how, as you move through your fears (any fear-based emotion), you naturally become one with the whole. Yet, in your growth and healing, you also are aware of who you are as a vital piece of the whole. You are a beautiful, magical human being in your true Soulful Self. By knowing your Self, you're better able to persevere through challenges in this life that otherwise may seem overwhelming and destructive.

But, as we've discussed, your truth has been elusive for the longest time. Growing up, you weren't taught to believe in your Self—you learned to accept what Other expects and wants you to believe. Those beliefs are not the truth of who you are. The idea is to learn to believe in you through your own perceptions of the experiences Other presented. This way, you can tease apart that upon which you've been built—and unearth your truth amid the tangled web of external teachings. You need to believe in your Self as separate from the lessons of your youth. How do you know who you are in truth beyond how Other defined you? How do you heal those areas where you do not "know" your Self?

When you look at TST, you see that the truth of who you are is love and that it's soulfully bound. In truth, you are love, and you are seeking love. You are so many beautiful characteristics—and more. Let's begin this process by looking at one experience.

Power is a love-based experience. Force is fear-based. Americans use the word power both ways, but in these teachings, power will be used as the gifted experience it is. To that end, begin by knowing that you are of a gracefully loving power. It's an energy that emanates from you and can be shadowed by your fear or the Other pocket. Take time to meditate on this. By becoming aware of the power that is in you, it allows you to feel a connection to your Soulful Self, and it opens the door for you to begin identifying truth of Self.

> *Exercise 6.1.* Focus on your breath. Breathe in and out. Follow your breath as it goes in and out. Do this at least four times. Become conscious of your breathing. Then breathe into your abdomen, right behind your belly button. As you pull your breath into your core, feel the expansiveness of you. Breathe in a soft golden white light, and feel it fill your abdomen and core. It is a graceful power of love. With each in-breath, feel your power as that soft golden white light, and allow it to fill your body, one breath at a time. Continue to focus on your breath pulling in the love that illuminates the power that is expanding to fill your body. First, you feel it in your lower abdomen, behind the belly button. Then that golden white light grows to fill your chest, warming your heart. Then it grows to fill your pelvis, feeling alive. The power grows to fill your head, releasing you of thought. Then it fills your arms and legs. Once you perceive the golden white light filling your being, feel it expand outward beyond your physical being. Be the golden white light as it moves beyond your physical being and expands 15 to 20 feet high and wide. Feel the shift in how you recognize the world around you when you're this large. Feel the graceful power that emanates love and acceptance, first for you and then for all else. It flows from you to all Other.

After the meditation, do you feel your Self energetically and physically? Probably. If you had a hard time meditating on your own, you can find this meditation on my website (kristenbomas.com). Sometimes a guided meditation can help you focus and experience.

Once you feel this experience you have a taste of your true Soulful Self. It allows you the opportunity to feel your graceful power, a power that gently emanates from you always. When you're aware of it, you can foster it. When you're not conscious of it, it can become force (that fear-based experience that pushes and pulls others from their free will or depletes belief in your Self). There are many fear-based experiences that are created when you're not in awareness of belief in your Self. But, in truth, you are a graceful, powerful being who has a beautiful inner description.

> *Exercise 6.2.* List all the things you do for others, and that you do in life, that you love about you. Do not judge the effort as egotistical. It's not. Take your time. List everything you can think of that you love about what you *do* in this life. Are you kind, helpful, caring, giving, accepting, etc.? Once you've made your list, read it knowing the following: If you are doing all this for others, then it's *who and what you are* in truth. You do not have to put effort into it. It always will be a part of you.

People tell me all the time that they are considerate of the way others feel, and that they do not want to be selfish (or some other set of characteristics). I find myself saying, "You are a thoughtful person! You would be thoughtful even if you didn't put effort into it. You are not a selfish person. That would take effort!" I also listen to people describe acts of kindness toward friends, family and strangers. When I ask, they say they do these things because they want to show they care. In truth, they are a very caring person and do not have to try so hard to show it. They would have to try very hard to NOT be kind!

Identify where you have similar thoughts. And be conscious of the above examples. You may believe you're doing these things because you want to be good enough. The truth of who you are, however, is the very thing you think you're doing to prove your Self as good enough to be loved. In other words, you're already good enough and lovable! It's the illusion of your fear—the fear of not being good enough—that drives you to "do" things that are inherent truths of who and what you are.

Remember, all fear-based beliefs or beliefs that do not enhance your love for your Self, are taught. There are six steps that you can use to dismantle those beliefs. See my small eBook, Unveil Your Truth: 6 Steps to Moving beyond Limiting Beliefs. It's important that you become aware of the beliefs that are not in harmony with your truth. It's here that much of your healing will occur.

KNOW YOUR EXPERIENCE

Once you begin believing in or knowing your Self, you have begun the process of knowing your experience. When you believe in your Self, you want to create greater happiness for your Self. You want "more" for yourself—more happiness, freedom, love, acceptance, etc. That is abundance. Every time you leave your Self to listen to another, you have entered "lack"—you are lacking Self in the equation! It's impossible to create abundance when you are lacking Self. Abundance flows to you, through you, from you. So, without You there is no flow experienced at that time.

It's imperative to your freedom in this life that you know *what it is that you wish to experience*. Otherwise, you are in the experience of Other not Self. Again, you are lacking Self and therefore cannot find freedom or abundance.

So, what kind of "experience" are we talking about? Could it be a wish for financial freedom? No. That's not an experience. That's a label of what you want to physically have, and it comes from what you have learned. You may even create a physical number that defines financial freedom.

Those labels and/or expectations are limiting. The real question involves what you wish to experience *on the inside*. If you had financial freedom, how would you know it? What would you be feeling and experiencing within your Self? This life is about the experience inside you. The more you are aware of your Soulful Self, the more you are aware of your experience. Likewise, the more you tend to the experience you are having, the more you tend to Self—and, consequently, to growing Self's presence in your life.

Using the above physical wish, let's go back to TST. It's important to know why you desire the experience. Start by listening to your desired experience. Is it external (Other) or internal (Self)? If you have defined a physical experience, it is external to Self. Therefore, you need to identify an internal desire to bring it over to the left-hand column. Ask yourself why you would like financial freedom. Do you have fears about not having enough money? Do you feel not good enough or insignificant without more money? Do you define personal success through financial freedom? What does being successful mean to you?

Some of you might wish to have financial freedom because you will feel successful. Some of you may want it to purchase a larger home (external object based upon social expectation)—but upon further exploration, it's really to feel safer (fear). Some of you may want it to have the freedom to move about this plane (love-based). Others of you may have different wants.

I've worked with many successful entrepreneurs and executives who keep upping their goals to redefine success. They don't have an internal definition of the experience of success; they're using external measures to prove they are good enough. But inside, they're afraid; no matter how much they achieve in business, they still don't *feel* good enough. They hope that scaling that next mountain—earning even more money, taking their company to the next level, accumulating more material (personal and/or business-related) possessions, driving a competitor out of the market—will alleviate this feeling. But it never does. They first must *believe* that they're good enough. Then, and only then, can they define the experience of success they wish to have. Once they define it as a love-based experience of Self, they're able to achieve business success on a much deeper and more gratifying level.

> **Exercise 6.3.** What is the experience of being successful that you're trying to achieve? Do you know? Write out your experience as you know it. An example might be living in a large home. You may see yourself in a relationship that is loving and fun, and where you do a lot together. You may see yourself driving the car of your dreams, or wearing designer, cutting-edge fashion. OK. But what are you really looking for? How will it feel to live in a large home? Will it have amenities? Which ones and why? What do each of the amenities bring to you in the way of internal experience. See yourself experiencing the home and its amenities (do not see yourself sharing them, just alone experiencing them). What does it feel like? What is the experience each amenity brings you? Imagine the home is on an island that no one knows about and that no one else will see. How do you feel living in the home and experiencing the amenities? Ask yourself similar questions for each of the characteristics you described as successful. You are beginning to understand what you wish to experience in life and what "successful" means to you.

Once you are done, reread your descriptions. When alone, what is the experience you wish to have? Are there still components of wanting others to approve or to see your accomplishments? If so, you know there is still an external "other" you wish to please. You can see that those parts are from the Other column; the aspects that are truly self-serving are from the Self column. This will help you begin to define Your experience rather than living out experiences defined by Other.

In love relationships, it is the same. Most of you do not know the experience you wish to have in an ideal relationship. You find yourself excited to experience love, and then you try to hold onto that. Using TST, you can see that you are excited by the external giving of love (Other) and that you are trying to hold onto "it" (attachment; fear-based emotion). Without knowing your experience, you can find yourself looking outward for fulfillment— but not knowing what fulfillment is.

CHAPTER

7

Speaking Your Truth— Embarking On Mastery

INTRODUCTION

The Sage observes. She is centered in her own experience. She knows her Self. She, therefore, sees other people and experiences for what they are because she sees the world from within. Her ego is mostly absent. Therefore, she does not have the need to tell others about themselves. She does not need others to agree with her and does not impose her opinions, assumptions, or expectations upon others. She is free from those restraints. She speaks from her inside experience without the need to affect Other. The Sage speaks her own truth.

The process of becoming a Sage is anchored in transcending the fear-based side of the Template and living in a state of love and truth. The Sage's Template™ uses language as a tool to help you begin conscious life mastery by identifying and shifting away from an egotistical life and unveiling freedom.

As mentioned earlier, most of you have the desire to be understood and heard by Other, to have an impact on the listener or environment. You have now learned that you must first know Self; only then can you teach Other who you are.

Until that time, the external world is operating off assumptions of who you are. The need to be known, and the yearning to have an impact, keep you attached to the external world. Therefore, you are more focused externally than internally. In doing that, you assume the reaction or response that you see in Other—and you use that assumption to move forward in your life.

The process involved with flipping the script—of reaching a point where you're now teaching Other who you are—invites a mastery of the very challenges that have blocked you from receiving and accepting this awareness. That takes communication with (and understanding of) Self, first. And, then, communication with all Other.

Thus, we begin a new style of communicating that supports (and is supported by) your journey to enlightenment.

Understanding the limitations inherent in your current communication can help you see where your language is from Other and not Self. It can reveal instances where you're interacting through Other (the larger pocket) instead of experiencing your truth. Awareness of your language, through communication, allows you to use the Template for mastery.

This chapter will help you observe your language through this prism. It runs concurrent with the unveiling of Self that occurs through use of the Template. To communicate in a style that speaks your truth, you first must be able to discern Self versus Other. You also must be present with Self to speak that truth spontaneously to all Other. You can move beyond all limitations inherent to our current style of communicating by using an awareness of Self and language of Self to present yourself to the world.

OVERVIEW OF COMMUNICATION

The circle of communication begins and ends with You. We are *always* communicating. We all communicate in life, in some form or another. Like life, communication can be physical or energetic in nature.

Energetic communication is the most unseen form of communication; it emanates from you and those around you. And it's a constant. Examples of energetic communication include: the way a child or an animal responds to a person and how they feel comfortable or uncomfortable based on their "sense" of that person and their presence; or how you can walk into a room and tell there is tension between the people who are in there.

Physical forms of communication, nonverbal and verbal, are more familiar. Nonverbal communication might be gestured, sexual, written, drawn, etc. Verbal communication can be spoken out loud or within your thoughts. Most programs focus on the verbal and follow it with body language. Yet, as you can see, there is so much more than language and body.

Language originates from the need to communicate. Therefore, it's important to know the origin of your communication. Is your language coming *from* Self or Other (who/what you learned from)? Are you communicating *about* Self or Other?

HOW YOU WERE TAUGHT TO COMMUNICATE

You learned to communicate from the beginning of this life. Communication began from the time you were attached to those around you. Your first language was emotion and intuition. For example, when you cried as an infant, your parent responded by feeding you or changing your diaper. Magic! Their energetic and physical response "said" you were safe. An absence of response "said" you were abandoned and not safe.

As you became more understanding of verbal communication, you spoke and received feedback in response to your words. During the terrible 2s, for example, a child learns that their language and actions impact all that's around them.

Growing up, you were told what to do, what to think, what to believe, and who you were to be (See Figure 16). Quickly, you learned to respond and interact with Other in a way that was pleasing to them. Why? Because you needed to feel accepted and wanted.

Initially, this tied into your survival instinct. But what about You? How are *you* going to be heard and understood? In this style of communicating, you learned to be physically acceptable—but not emotionally and uniquely accepted. Is this where you bought into your perception that you were not good enough to be loved? Does that fear then influence your communication? Absolutely. You want to be accepted, understood, good enough, and loved.

Is your style of communicating bringing those experiences to you?

INFLUENCES IN LEARNED COMMUNICATION

The greatest influences in your current style of communicating were the external sources from your past (parents, peers, society, etc.), Other, that told you what to do and who to be. For the most part, no one was asking about you. Instead, you were taught to listen to what Other said—and respond accordingly. You learned to please Other in order to be accepted. You learned to live based on an external focus and expectations. You learned to look to Other for reward. As you were communicating, you learned that what you wanted needed to match what they wanted for you.

> *Example 7.1.* Sami walks into a room where her parents are in conversation with another couple. She is asked what she wants to do when she grows up. She says, "I am going to be a firefighter!" The adults in the room think it is so "cute." Yet, no one takes the time to follow up with Sami and learn why she wants to be a firefighter. Sami walks away feeling good and rewarded that everyone thought her idea was cute. But she didn't learn to explore her own Self and why she wants to be a firefighter—because no one asked. She didn't learn that others are interested in *who she is*.

If this example resonates, then you did not learn how to know your experience OR how to speak about your Self. Instead, what people know about you is what they assume about you.

The way you learned to communicate forced you to have an external focus. As a result, you stopped putting your Self at the core of your communication with Other. Instead, you learned to tell someone what you want them to do, change, or say to, hopefully, make you feel better. It feels more "natural" than to say how *you* feel and what *you* need in order to create a better experience.

> *Example 7.2.* James was getting increasingly frustrated by the household chores he was doing; he'd rather share that time with his partner. Instead, it seemed that the chores were a "job." He would drop hints, but he didn't know how to express to his partner what he really felt. One day he got frustrated and said, "You never clean up or help around the house! Why can't we do this together?"

His partner said, "I do help! I just did the lawn!"

James responded, "You chose to do that because you like it. That isn't helping ME around here. Do you think this is my job? I work full time too!"

His partner replied, "You don't appreciate anything I do."

As you can see, James did not attain a sharing of tasks that he thought would be positive for him in the relationship. His partner doesn't understand James' true feelings—or from where they originated. Instead, his partner thinks nothing he does is good enough. His partner thinks this is about him; he has no idea it's about James. The partner has no idea that James feels unappreciated because *he* is now feeling unappreciated! The partner may start asking James if he can help, but he does not know that he is sharing to bring joy to James' life. He doesn't know about James' needs; he's just doing what was asked to try to make James happy.

You can see how this sets a stage for another frustration for James down the road because he hasn't satisfied his need to be known and understood.

The external influence of communication has James telling his partner (Other) about him and speaking from his fear/expectations rather than his love. Both of those pieces are insidiously woven into your communication style. It forces you out of the Self pocket and into the Other pocket (See Figure 11 on page 17.) Focusing on the external clearly limits your expression of Self.

LIMITATIONS IMPOSED BY AN EXTERNAL FOCUS

By looking outward, toward Other, life is limited. By looking inward, toward Self, the possibilities are infinite, possibilities that you can experience.

Because the Sage sees everything from the inside out, she does not see limitations in any Other. We now understand that the communication you've been taught focuses on Other; consequently, it imposes limits. The circle of communication, however, begins and ends with you. Therefore, it is about you—and from you. Communication can open you beyond the limitations and take you to the infinite.

Instead of exploring your Self and your world, you've learned to read the expectations of you by Other. In addition to being limiting, responding to those expectations (or doing whatever needs to be done to meet them) also breeds fear.

You learn to live from assumptions rather than looking for and expressing true experiences. You then use assumptions to define Other and relationships with Other. Your assumptions, however, come from you and are filtered through your past and your perceptions. They are not the truth (or even the intention) of Other until you ask. Assumptions about you do not accommodate your changes in life, or your truth. It's a place where you can feel unknown and unheard. Often, I hear people say they know someone better than that person knows their self! That's impossible. Your assumption is limiting that person to *who you think he or she is!* The same limitations exist against you when Other assumes you are who they think you are. This is why some parents don't really *know* their child, even though they think they do.

You learn to doubt who you are, which, again, is very limiting. You learn the shame that comes from Other judging and seeing you as different than who you know your Self to be. That's limiting. The judgments that Other puts upon you in life come from their fears of being judged. These insidious shaming judgments can instill doubt; this not only prevents you from being you in the moment, but it can impose limitations on the future expression of you.

Against this backdrop, you learned not to explore your Self, let alone teach others about your Self. Consequently, you learned to respond to Other instead of talking about your Self. Even when you did talk about you, it was often in response to (or out of respect for) Other.

As a child your natural curiosity takes you inside yourself. Children tend to be creative and inquisitive. They do not fear what they will find. But you were taught to fear your inner search thanks to judgments and expectations that were put upon you. That fear was born out of the assumptions of Other. You felt the need to meet their expectations because their assumptions about you must have had value, right? At least that's what you learned. Thus, many of you stopped your creative search of Self and listened to what you were told.

You learned to speak in order to be received—not to be understood. In turn, there was no correlation between being understood and being accepted. You can see how this limits your freedom to speak spontaneously about your inner experience. If you feel hesitant to speak of your true experience, then you are stopping your Self from being fully present. True acceptance is felt when you are present and when you experience the acceptance of your truth.

You learned to be invested in what they tell you because their voice must have importance. Growing up you knew you needed to be accepted by them because you could not survive on your own. In that light, you likely mimicked their view of you to stay safe—and you probably avoided things that you understood might upset them. Along the way, you learned to tell people about Other rather than teaching people about you. By telling others about them, you become so limited that you're virtually left out of the equation.

A quick aside: Let's say you do address Other about who they are, or something they did. It's likely Other will become defensive. Once there is defensiveness, preservation of Self kicks in. A battle against the perceived threat ensues, but the Self is hidden during that battle.

You learned to speak in order to influence Other. That limits you to what you want THEM to learn rather than having a voice on behalf of Self. It's not your job to change someone's mind or influence them in a direction that you feel is better. That is ego. Your heart is in the right place, but it's still the ego that needs to influence Other. Where there is ego, there is an absence of truth of Self. Remember, the ego is the persona of fear, and fear is of Other—not Self.

It's important to note that not everyone experiences the scope of these learnings. Some people can recognize the limitation, but they may not have complete awareness of its existence in every aspect of their life. Not all of these learnings occur consciously; some subtly filter into our lives or arrive through observation. That is why many of you can identify with or understand the limitations.

Most of you wish to be heard and known for who YOU are. Therefore, communication needs to be from you, of you, and about you before it is about Other. Obviously, that is not the way you learned to communicate. You learned to communicate to others based upon *their* expectations, thus creating the aforementioned external focus. Without you as the core, communication breaks down and leads to breakdown in relationships—all relationships. Without you as the core, relationships can't open you and Other, and deepen the bond and freedom; instead, they limit and slowly divide your connection.

It's a wonder you are understood at all. You're aching to be heard and understood for who you are, but you have learned to communicate about Other to Other. You couldn't advocate for Self, let alone speak about or learn about Self, because you were too busy learning about Others' expectations and perceptions. In the meantime, they were so busy telling you who and what you are, that they didn't give you the tools to explore your life and find out who you are.

It's no surprise that people are insecure about expressing their needs and desires, in this light, given the fears of judgment, rejection, or destruction.

CONCLUSION

As we can now see, you were taught to communicate by looking outward at Other, assuming their expectations, and then attempting to meet or change those expectations. The way you were taught to communicate imposes significant limitations on you and your relationships. Because you were taught to look outward at Other, you have experienced many defensive reactions regarding Other.

You were telling them about them, however, with the hopes that if *they* change, you will feel better. You can see how limiting that is and how many blocks and illusions there are to you finding happiness. That type of communicating sets the stage for offense-defense. It's not an opening of you about you to Other. Nor is it a curiosity about Other that asks them to teach you about their Self or purpose.

So, let's discuss how you can communicate in a way that opens you and your relationships to greater freedom in life. Let's look at how communication can open you to mastery of your challenges and of life.

COMMUNICATING FROM SELF: A CONSCIOUS EXPRESSION OF LIFE MASTERY

UNDERSTANDING YOUR SELF

By now, you realize that Self-discovery is the cornerstone of this journey. Knowing your Self is the key to being understood the way you wish to be known. Knowing your Self includes moving beyond some of the communication styles previously discussed, as well as transcending the fears and concerns that resulted from that communication.

To know your Self is to know how you feel at any given moment, as well as what you are experiencing and what you wish to be experiencing. As noted in other chapters, we define life through how we feel about it. Consequently, to communicate your Self to Other, it's vital to understand your Self and what you wish to experience (versus what you are experiencing). You want to know where there is harmony between the two and where there is discord.

Begin by becoming aware of your emotions.

Whether you are aware of your emotions or not, they always influence your communication. Recall that emotions (prior to being felt) are energy and are a constant. They are the language that tells you where you are feeling the truth of who and what you are (love-based and Self) versus the fear-based challenges (like anger, guilt, shame) put upon you by Other. Many people are not aware of their emotions until they are felt. But you can gain an awareness of how you're feeling in any situation by understanding your background thoughts or intention.

Over the years of learning to communicate, you were gaining information about your Self based on how Other perceived you, or how Other wanted you to be. However, *you are you*! Uniquely and beautifully YOU.

So, what were the beliefs from Other that pushed you further from your truth? Did you adopt the religion in which you were raised? Or were you given a choice of a religion that fit you best? Were you presented with a style of clothes? Or did you create your own style? Did anyone influence your decisions about education or work? How about your partner in life? Those in the LGBTQA family know all too well what it's like to have to buy into a lifestyle that's inconsistent with who you are. For the rest of you, it may not have been so obvious; perhaps, gradually and over time, it just became a part of your everyday expression.

Growing up, you were exploring life and your Self, but you may have been limited in how to share what you found. Most people were trying to be what Other wanted them to be. That's because much of our learning had to do with "what was right for you" in accordance with family, religious, community, or educational (Other) views approved by your parents. To that end, you were pushed to observe what Other expected and to communicate accordingly.

For example, sometimes children will tell white lies because they are afraid of getting in trouble if they tell the truth. Then, one day, they are called a liar. They may begin to believe, or buy into the idea, that they are a liar—and, thus, are bad—all because they feel they can't tell the truth without being criticized. It's a double-edged sword. The child makes an agreement with the experiences, one that continues to influence communication and relationships as they move on in life.

This old style of communicating forms many beliefs about ourselves. Yet none of it is who we are! You *know* the truth of who you are and the discordance with what Other told you to be. Because of this constant incongruence, many of you have found your Self fighting to be heard or known. This is why people become defensive within this style of communicating. Others are telling you what you did, what your intention was, what you really meant, etc.

There are many agreements (or beliefs) created between parent and child through the years. It's up to you to begin to recognize the beliefs, patterns and teachings that came from Other during your childhood and formative years. Why is this recognition, and the understanding that comes with it, so important? These are the tools that will enable you to communicate in a more profound, enlightened, and honest manner moving forward. That's because you'll be communicating the truth of who you are.

LISTENING TO YOUR SELF: OBSERVING SELF

You are not what you were told (Other), but you may not be wholly who you are (SelfOther). So, when you are communicating, how are others learning about you? Or are they? Often, I hear from clients that they do not feel heard and/or understood. They attribute that to the other person not listening.

But are you listening to You? And what does that really mean? Do you listen to your thoughts or to the words that leave your mouth? Do you listen to You, and your dreams and desires? Do you "listen" for where there is a conflict between how you feel and what you are doing or saying?

It's essential that you listen to your Self. To be inwardly aware of your experience and emotions will open you to your Self. The more you know of your Self and listen to its language, the more you can teach Other. Train your Self to be aware of your inner experience by identifying where you feel comfortable and where you feel uncomfortable.

If you know you're feeling comfortable and happy, or if you enjoy what you are hearing or experiencing, state it clearly and watch how other people respond in likeness. Why? Because your words echo your inner self or energy; and people pick up on that. This is what makes a person feel genuine and transparent.

If someone steps on your toe with their high heel, you say, "Ouch!" Similarly, if someone says something that hurts, you can say, "Ouch! That hurt!" It's rare that the other person will become defensive because, again, you are coming across as genuine. You're not telling the other person something bad about them. It's just that the high heel hurt!

That inner awareness of listening also includes your voice. Becoming aware of your voice and its message helps to shed light on what's going on inside. Feel from where your voice originates. Your voice can range from being pinched and tight (coming from the very top of your "throat") to being open and free (coming from your diaphragm). This tells you where you are cut off from your truth and where you are speaking from your truth, respectively. Obviously, there are various "voices" in between the two edges.

Here is an exercise to practice that will teach you to open your voice from your diaphragm.

Exercise 7.1.

- With your finger pointed, stretch out your arm so that your finger is as high as the tip of your head.
- Now, take a deep breath and as you slowly release it let a note or sound come up the back of your throat, along the roof of your mouth and "hit" your finger! You are singing the note into your fingertip.
- You will begin to feel the shift in your voice as it begins to come from deep within you.
- Now practice speaking a sentence from that same point.

If you don't hear or feel your inner emotions as others speak to you (or if you think you are hiding those emotions when you speak to someone), your communication is going to be skewed. The other person will detect the incongruence between emotional and verbal expression. As you learn to listen to who you are—beyond the cacophony of voices from Other that tell you who to be, how to be, and what is right and what is wrong—you will realize what you want others to hear.

What you want them to hear is who you are, what you believe, what experiences you wish to have—and so much more!

By learning to observe and listen to your Self, you're redirecting the focus away from external opinions, judgments, and thoughts learned from Other. Instead, you're staying within your own experience. This can lead to you watching *how Other speaks*.

As you learn to create the position of observer, rather than student, you begin taking things less personally—or not personally at all. You stop absorbing the words that are spoken; instead, you observe the words and how they are spoken. Being aware of your inner experience as the observer and Self, you're now prepared to speak in response to Other, as opposed to reacting to Other. In the process, you're allowing the healing of challenges to occur or to continue. Ultimately, this will lead to clearer communication from you and about you to others. It will allow you to speak from your truth without worry of the response or reaction of Other to your words.

As you learn to observe your Self, you will stay more present in the communication. Eventually, you will be able to see what is truly of you, and what was learned or put upon you. At that point, you'll be able to spontaneously speak your inner truth.

To succeed at listening and observing your Self, you also must learn to not judge your Self. Just listen and observe!

SPEAKING YOUR TRUTH

SPEAKING FROM AND ABOUT SELF

Speaking from your true Self requires an ability to observe the difference between Self and Other, Truth and Illusion. Once the observing has helped you feel the difference, you will want to share the truth of your inner experience. This is what I call learning to speak your truth.

The goal is to learn to speak of you and from you, as if there is no one else. In other words, allow your Self the opportunity to be observing, understanding, and accepting of you. Does that sound like there are two of you? Perhaps there are.

You, the Self. And you, the observer of Self.

It's difficult for my clients (and I would imagine most of you) to speak only of themselves. Most want to include Other. Some want to focus on Other. But communication must begin with you—and be about you—in order for other people to know who you are. How else are they going to learn about you as a different and unique being? It's what most people ultimately want out of communication: to be heard and understood.

Do you want people to know you only because of your achievements, their assumptions, or other people's descriptions of you? Or, do you want people to learn who you truly are because of what you teach them?

Let me give you an example.

> **Example 7.3**. A woman is in a marriage, and she's frustrated. Every morning the childcare is her sole responsibility while her partner sleeps in. One morning she says, "When are you going to take some responsibility, wake up early, and take care of your children? You are a parent too! I'm tired and frustrated. And I feel unappreciated!"

It sounds like she taught Other about her Self, right? But she probably didn't. Other probably heard: "She thinks I'm not doing enough even though I go to work every day and bring in the money that pays the bills. She thinks I'm lazy and ungrateful!"

If that's what is heard, then the partner is feeling defensive. If the partner is feeling defensive, then he or she did not hear anything except criticism of not doing enough or doing it right. The woman walks away unheard and the partner walks away unappreciated.

If, however, she had said, "I am exhausted, and I need help. I find myself getting frustrated inside and then my thoughts lead me to feeling unappreciated," her partner would be able to hear her experience and her desire. The partner now understands what can be done to help her feel supported.

It takes learning to know who you are and how you are really feeling. That leads to knowing what you wish to experience and, from there, you can communicate your Self and your experience to another. Sounds like a lot, right? Not really.

Take a minute and observe that sentence within your Self. It is *all* already happening, always. It's a matter of you tuning into it (that is, the observing and listening described in the previous section). Now that you can "see" and "hear" Self, you must verbalize Self to Other. You are now ready to see the magic of your relationships begin!

Let's review communication of Self. Learning who you are and expressing that truth to others is of critical importance. It sets you free from the limitations that were imposed on you. Most of you learned to communicate in absence of that truth of Self. You learned to communicate by watching others and learning about them so that you could read their expectations and meet or exceed them.

That style of communicating keeps you looking at Other and assuming the answer or what "should" be said. It also keeps you attached to Other's response or reaction.

Mastery is about knowing your Self, listening to your Self, and observing your Self. Those qualities also are critical to communicating your Self—thoughts, dreams, and desires—to Other. You can start to see why The Sage's Template™ uses language as its source for conscious healing and transforming. The teachings enable you to begin speaking *of* your Self *from* your Self. This way, you feel supported, heard, and understood.

Now let's address the new style of speaking with others.

TEACHING OTHER ABOUT YOU

Imagine that life is like a matrix, an infinite matrix. Each crosshatch in the matrix is a challenge, and each challenge is another matrix. Consequently, your life is an infinite web of matrices, and you exist in the center. The same example applies to every individual. So, if you don't know your Self, how can you know other people? Likewise, if others don't know themselves, how can they be expected to know you? You must become the expert of you and allow others to become the experts of themselves.

Knowing your inner experience, whatever it may be, and then being able to express it to Other is critical to your freedom. Speaking your truth means saying what YOU are experiencing. It's NOT about your opinion of Other, or your solution for Other, or anything else that includes Other.

It's about you.

There is only one person in the Template, and that person is YOU. That said, you still need to understand the Other pocket so that you can move beyond your challenges—and unveil your truth. Your truth will set you free. As you teach Other about you, you are actively voicing the challenge that you are healing, or the truth you are unveiling. It's the truth of where you are in your experience of life in that moment. It's saying, "This is where the past is keeping me from the present (challenges put upon this life by Other), and this is where I am present (Soulful Self, freedom)."

OVERVIEW OF STRUCTURE

As described in previous sections, you learned to communicate by Other telling you what to think, say, feel, and be. That is what constructed your Other pocket, the pocket of challenges that defined this life. It's what hid your truth, your Soulful Self.

If you want others to know about you, you must teach them. You must be the originator of the communication about you. Furthermore, you must know what it is about you that you want them to know or understand. In that model, you are telling others about the truth, as you know it, of who you are, what you're currently experiencing, or what you wish to experience. Communication about you needs to begin and end with you. It looks like this (Figure 17):

Remember, it's not about their agreement with or approval of what you are saying. It's about your ability to be the expert about you. If you are an Olympic gold medalist in snowboarding, are you going to be influenced by the opinions and judgments of a man who has never been on a snowboard? Probably not. Why, then, would you listen to opinions and judgments of YOU by Other? No one knows you or what it is like inside you. So, express that. Describe you to Other. This style of communicating puts you in the expert's position.

TEACHING ABOUT YOUR SELF AND EXPLORING ALL OTHER

More than a century ago, advertisers peddled cocaine as a tooth-soothing medication. There also was a time when beer companies promoted their product as being good for pregnant women. Soda companies delivered a similar message, touting the benefits of soft drinks for young children. Back in the day, such "wisdom" was endorsed by the experts of that time. Of course, through advancements in science and research, we now know better.

Similarly, you are accumulating knowledge by embarking on this journey and using the Template. Don't judge where you've been, or your lack of knowledge about who you really are. What you do know is what's relevant. Teach others what you know, and that will open doors that allow you to know your Self better. You're constantly changing. So will the knowing of your Self.

Let's look at an example.

> **Example 7.4.** A woman expresses to her husband that she's in need of some calm and loving days in order to feel affectionate. He responds by becoming angry. He insists on affection while telling her that she has no intention of being affectionate with him, and that she doesn't care about him. She defends her feelings for him and tells him that she does love him, and that she didn't intend to make him angry with her need.

The conversation is now about him being upset—and her trying to soothe him. She is no longer the focus. Both parties are looking at Other (remember, this is your challenge pocket). He sees judgment of him not being good enough; she is placating him without getting the response that she wants. Both have lost touch with the experience they truly desire.

He felt scared when she said she needed more calm and love; he thought that meant he wasn't doing enough in the relationship. Instead of telling her that the comment scared him, he told her about *how she feels*—despite the fact that she clearly stated how she feels and what she wants. To complicate matters, she forgot her clearly stated desire when she focused, instead, on his opinions about her and what he thought she was feeling.

In the end, it was all about taking care of him. She walked away further disappointed and feeling alone. He walked away with lingering feelings that she doesn't care about him.

Now, let's redo the example (and switch the roles) with each person teaching about their Self and see where it goes.

The man clearly states that he misses affection in their relationship; he wishes to see more calm and loving expression so that he feels affectionate again. The woman responds to him by teaching that she doesn't understand: Does he think it's all her or that there is something they are doing that needs to be identified?

She continues to say that she feels hurt because her thoughts are going to fears of not being good enough; she describes how, at that point, she becomes afraid he will leave her. She states that she misses the affection as well. He then responds to her by saying, "You ARE good enough, and you are the only woman I wish to be with. But when there's constant anger and tension in the household, I pull back and don't want to go forward. I need your help feeling safe at those times."

She understands and responds, "I too need your help with my fears of not being good enough and feeling like I have lost you when you pull back."

They've each learned about the other while deepening the intimacy of their relationship.

When you are teaching others about your Self, you are not telling them about them. You are staying centered in your own Self and what you wish to experience or what you are experiencing. You are responsible for your own life and your reactions to life unfolding around you. You don't need to focus on how your truth is or isn't received. The other person, meanwhile, is responsible for their own life and their reactions to life around them. Learn to let go of the need to take responsibility for Other's reactions or responses to your experiences. This is the beginning of not taking things personally.

Example 7.5. Dan is an executive for a large company. One day, he's in a meeting with the officers and vice presidents. One of the vice presidents states that he didn't receive in time the numbers he needed from Dan to update a project. Dan had not given him a deadline because it wasn't his project; the vice president needed to communicate that Dan had a deadline. Dan felt publicly called out and shamed. He felt the colleague should have come to him separately. He wanted to tell the other person what he did wrong and how he could address a situation like that in the future.

A part of him also wanted to make himself feel better and "defend" his reputation by telling everyone in the room what this vice president had done. Instead, once he recognized the importance of speaking his truth rather than blurting out the story, he went to the colleague and voiced his discomfort with the public statement. He asked to be addressed privately and directly if the vice president felt, moving forward, that he failed to deliver in any way. The colleague was genuinely apologetic—and he opened up about his discomfort with going to others when they do something wrong. Both parties grew from the episode.

By learning to teach people about your Self, you become aware that others are always teaching you about them! Even though they think they are teaching you about you! By teaching others, you also are discovering who wants to learn about you and who wants to stay in their assumptions about you (regardless of how different their opinion is compared to what you're attempting to teach them). This leads to greater awareness in a relationship.

To teach others about your Self, you must be willing to explore your Self. That means delving into what you feel and desire, and what you wish to experience. The more you're willing to explore your Self and your true existence, the more you'll be able to teach others about you.

As you become familiar with asking your Self what you are feeling or experiencing, you become more adept at asking questions involving exploration. Trying similar questions in conversation with other people. Of course, your exploration will differ depending on whether you're conversing with a business colleague or a life partner.

But when you explore Other, use open questions; allow them to offer their words and their unique way of expressing. Otherwise, you're not exploring them. Pointed questions can be a form of interrogating them. You're trying to see if they'll give you the answer for which you're looking. When you're exploring another person genuinely and with compassion, you're asking them what something means to them, what they are thinking, or what they're working to experience. You're exploring their inner world. You are letting go of the ego that says it needs to know or it needs to be right.

You are stepping into their world to see it through their eyes.

If you can do this, and become the observer of Other, you'll find that you don't take anything they say personally. If Other is genuinely exploring themselves to answer your questions about them, then they are looking to truly unveil themselves to you. If they're giving you a defensive answer that is directed at you (perhaps, one that's even hurtful)—and you're in the position of observer—you will see how they struggle and suffer in their life. Over time, and with practice, you'll learn to not take it personally.

It doesn't matter how much you think you already "know" about why another person acts the way they do or believes the things you perceive they believe. It matters that you are willing to *ask* them, with compassion, what makes them tick and what is going on inside them at a given time. What is going on inside them at a given time. By gaining the willingness to learn about Other, you open your Self to their infinity. The more you ask Other about their true Self, the more you see how much there is to learn. It also confirms that you are in need of being known by you; thus, you will explore your Self more as well.

UNRAVELING THE FOUR CHARACTERISTICS OF MISCOMMUNICATION

There are four elements in communication that can lead to miscommunication, creating limitations to, and dividing, your relationship with all Other:

1) Telling others about who they are and trying to influence them
2) Assumptions
3) Expectations
4) Perceptions

You have relationships to expand your life—not limit it. Yet, so often, you may feel hindered or trapped by your relationship with Other. Perhaps, you feel stuck in your relationship with Self, your career, life, your partner, family, etc. You don't feel fulfilled or joyous. You feel the struggles rather than the passion. Remember, you are always communicating—and you are always in relationship. Thus, it's important to see the connection between elements that cause miscommunication and your challenges in this life.

As you work through the challenges, you unveil the truth of your Self. Along the way, you're changing. So, throughout the journey, speak from your Self. Your observation of Self helps you become aware of where you're not being understood, and where you've stopped exploring life and Other around you.

Each of these four elements exist in communication from you and from those around you. As you become aware of your Self and your language, you will observe the use of these elements in others. This creates further awareness and enhances your ability to communicate about your Self—and to communicate with Other. Moving beyond the elements of miscommunication also allows you to rise above the tendency to take things personally. You're better equipped to read life and Other events—and to use those opportunities for growth.

TELLING OTHER ABOUT THEM

What makes you or someone else defensive in an interaction? Being told why you act a certain way? Being painted in a light that you don't believe is true? Being told that you are someone you're not? That your intentions weren't what they really were? When others *tell you about you*, chances are high that you'll feel defensive. The same holds true when you tell others about them.

If you can become aware of the fact that you are defensive, you may want to take a break from the conversation and ask your Self what triggered the defensiveness. Once you identify it, go back to the other person and say something like, "I found myself getting defensive when I heard _____. Could you please explain what you intended me to hear?" If you can become aware that the other person may be defensive, you might want to say, "I didn't mean to make you defensive, I truly meant ____."

If someone says something mean or hurtful to you, watch them and listen with your eyes not your ears. See what you think may be going on inside THEM. Then you can ask. If, however, someone is hurtful and thinks it's OK to hurt you with their words, do not attempt to engage. A great line is, "Ouch! That hurts!" You can't change that person. Just take care of you! It's *never* OK to be hurtful with words. It's never OK to be intentionally hurtful toward another in any way. That kind of communication often is part of an abuse pattern, which is a difficult pattern to break.

When you tell others about them, your ego is active. You are participating in a style of communicating that you were taught. No one is learning about you in that communication, and you are not learning about another. Move beyond your need to comment and open up your desire to ask and explore. Feel that within your Self. When others genuinely ask you about you, it feels grand. When they judge you or tell you about you, it feels terrible. When you tell another person about them, it's also inherently judgmental. That's why they take it personally when it comes from you—and why you take it personally when it comes from them.

When you master the art of staying the observer of Self and Other, you understand that someone telling you about you is really *them telling you about them*. Therefore, you see your Self telling them about them as your ego and not your truth. You will feel the absence of your Self internally. As you observe your Self and Other, you keep the exploration of Self and Other alive because you are constantly differentiating Self versus Other.

ASSUMPTIONS

Often, people assume thoughts, responses, etc., by Other. You learned to base your communication on assumption from the beginning. One way you learned that is by Other assuming you fit into their definition of you in childhood, and also by observing Other making assumptions about Other. As long as you assume another's response, thought, etc., you are playing out the communication and the relationship within your own head. The other person doesn't even have to be there! How often have you heard someone say something like, "I'm not going to invite [so and so] because they won't come anyway"? It's a classic assumption, and it runs the risk of that uninvited person feeling left out when they realize the event occurred without them.

Your assumptions are formed by your thoughts and past experiences. Assumptions are never about the other until you have confirmed them with the other. Furthermore, your assumptions of another keep that person in a fixed point and time. Assumptions do not allow for that person's change or growth.

What if you take the assumptions in your head, and you use them as opportunities to ASK the other person about them? What if you just invite the person in the above example to the event—and allow them to participate in the answer? Start asking people about their experience even if you think you know the answer. Ask them what they are experiencing when they are doing something. Ask them why they are feeling the way they are? Doors will open. Hearts will open. And communication will be enhanced.

Once you're comfortable exploring Other, it's time to become aware of your own assumptions. They can become a great source of exploration questions. Here's an example.

> *Example 7.6.* I was in the pool meditating one day while the man I was dating was in his garage working on his antiques (his hobby). As I was meditating, I had a clear picture of him at his workbench. He had a clear mind and a calm, peaceful inner experience. He was very focused. It was as if his hobby gave him a similar experience to my meditations. When I was done in the pool, I showered and dressed, and went to his work room to sit with him.
>
> I asked what his inner experience was while he was working at his bench. He thought for a bit and then said, "It's very quiet and peaceful. I'm focused yet there is nothing in my mind. It is clear. I would imagine it's a lot like when you meditate. … I can remember when my father would be at his bench, and I would be next to him." He then reminisced about his father for about 20 minutes, which took him deeper into his Self and his memories.
>
> What a gift! Had I walked out and stated my assumption, "When you are working on your antiques, do you get a calm peaceful feeling inside with a clear mind?" He would have said, "Yes." End of story. My ego would have been stroked, but I wouldn't have learned more about him. Because I explored him with an open question, he explored himself—and I received a wonderful gift!

Using assumptions as grist for the mill of exploratory questions moves you beyond telling others about them. It provides a window to genuinely observe and learn about them—from them. You also can use the assumptions to teach you about you. For example, if you're more comfortable not extending an invitation because you assume a person is going to say no, ask your Self why? Are you feeling fearful of the rejection? Are you frustrated by the relationship in some way? Or is there another experience occurring inside you that's limiting you from freely expressing your thoughts to that person?

See how limiting and debilitating assumptions can be to communication?

EXPECTATIONS

Next, let's look at the expectations by which you learned to live. What if you could become aware of those and use them as opportunities for growth and questions? For example, a parent looks at their child and says, "I expect you to keep your room clean! This is a disgrace!" The parent is reacting out of their own discomfort with the room's appearance, with lack of obedience in the child, with the disrespect of the home, and who knows what else.

That is what the parent is experiencing. The parent does not know what the child is doing until he or she *asks*! What happens that the room becomes so messy? Does the child like it? Does it allow the child to hide? Is it the one area the child screams rebellion? Or leave me alone? Or let me do things my way? Or is the room a reflection of how your child feels inside? There are myriad things that the child could be expressing through a disorganized, cluttered room. By throwing out the expectation, the parent or nanny is closing doors to the child's experience—and basing everything on their own experience and what they want their child to be.

Again, this is how you learned to communicate while growing up.

Expectations are always external to truth, but they show in a couple of ways. You could be watching to read what other people expect of you—and then say and or do what you think they expect. You also can have expectations attached to what you say. Or you can have expectations attached to how Other responds to what you say.

Expectations appear in language through the terms "expect," "should," "need to," "have to," and "supposed to." Anytime you hear yourself using any of those words out loud or in your thoughts, you are imposing expectations on Other or Self, respectively. As we learned earlier, anytime you use those words on Self, you are imposing expectations learned by Other. You never have expectations of Self. You have goals for Self. Once the expectations are removed, you are freeing Other to teach you about them and thus opening the relationship with Other. This also is true about the expectations in your thoughts about YOU.

While it may appear that the expectations are coming from you, they are learned from Other. More often than not, they originate from your challenges. So, when you use them in communication, you are not opening your Self (nor are you opening Other) to exploration. In fact, you are closing the door on possible opportunities. Expectations are limiting you, your life, and your relationships until you choose to become aware of them and use them to explore Self and Other.

There's an incongruence regarding what you wish to do or experience and what you think is expected of you. For example, some people love to make their bed in the morning. Some do not. Of those who do not, some will make their beds just because they "should." If that person were to ask their Self why they don't enjoy making the bed, they may learn something about their Self rather than living with the frustration of doing something that goes against their comfort. The general question is: What is the incongruence between what the expectation dictates and what you truly wish to be doing?

Moving beyond expectation is critical to acceptance of Self and Other. It allows you to explore the reason why a person is *not* doing what you expected them to do (or *not* being who you expected them to be). Where is the discord between the inner desire and the need for an expectation? When you hear your Self using an expectation, explore why "it" is not happening without an expectation.

Expectations can be part of assumptions and the need to tell others what to do, think, be and more. The combination creates the quiet and not-so-quiet thoughts of those learned challenges that so deeply limited you or stopped you from being all that you are.

PERCEPTIONS

Perceptions are formed within your Self, and they stem from your history. They are influenced by your unresolved challenges. As a result, perceptions are skewed. It's important, therefore, to learn that you are perceiving others, that others are perceiving you, *and* how to communicate in a way that allows perceptions to be an active part of your teaching and learning processes of communication.

If you are communicating with Other, there are perceptions occurring in a conscious and/or subconscious way. There are four parts to perception in communication. Those perceptions, like communication, begin with you. You are aware of you. Therefore, perception begins with your perception of your Self. Then you have a perception of the person across from you. Add to that, your perception of their perception of you. The fourth part is the actual experience or perceptions that are occurring in Other, about which you do not know.

That seems like a lot! But, wait, you're not done. There is another person (or more)! That other person has an awareness of what they are experiencing or perceiving. They are also perceiving you. They are perceiving your perception of them. Unknown to them is your perception and experience inside you.

As if that is not enough, there is one more critical point. Perceptions are anchored in *your* history of experiences.

For example, imagine someone mentions snow, and there are three people of various backgrounds listening. The first person has never seen snow; they may have a perception of it as beautiful but without the details that accompany an actual sensory experience. The second person flies to Colorado every spring and skis before returning home to Florida; their perception of snow is exciting and fun, refreshing and rejuvenating, etc. The third person is from Minnesota; they've experienced horrible winter storms, treacherous driving conditions, and frigid temperatures that cut you to the bone when going outside. That person associates snow with feelings of dread and apprehension. In this case, Other is a weather condition—but there are three very different perceptions.

If Other is a person, there are multiple dynamics. Each dynamic perceived by the observer carries its own history and meaning or feeling. It's truly a wonder that we communicate. Yet, we do.

If you are observing your Self and Other while communicating, you can become aware of perceptual differences and shifts in the communication. This takes knowing your Self, practicing, and exploring. The more you choose to master your challenges and life, the more your perceptions will become clear. Remember, any lack of clarity is due to your history and what you learned. As you master this life, you are undoing what Other put upon you and opening to your wisdom. This is the common truth and so you are moving beyond fear-based influences—those experiences that skew perception and, consequently, communication.

Perception is always active and influencing communication. When you're communicating with others, perceptions are influenced by more than just words—your nonverbal communication and most of your thoughts also play into perceptions. Additionally, as we perceive, we are usually assuming. You listen to your perceptions, and from that, you create assumptions about Other. Because assumptions are influenced by your perceptions, they are also anchored in your own history. As previously discussed, most people rely on their assumptions, more than the words of someone else, to direct them.

Your assumptions are frequent, and your perceptions are constant. Consequently, if you are also telling another about them, your perceptions are coming from you and your history. You're not really telling them much about them. Your perceptions, much like your assumptions, are a fertile ground for exploration questions. It's also a great opportunity to teach. If I have a friend who seems closed to meeting people, I may mention that to her. For example, I may say, "You feel very closed right now. Are you comfortable with meeting people?" You can see how the first part addresses my perception, and the second addresses my assumption.

While assumptions and perceptions are happening inside you there is another component that also may be active: expectations! Each expectation is perceived in some way. Each has a perceptual influence on your communication with Other. Your perceptions may house what you think Other expects of you. You also may expect something out of Other. If you expect someone to do something, you may be assuming that they perceive things as do you.

Can you see the chaos that can ensue in such communication?

Here's an example.

A housekeeper periodically asks the homeowner if she can move her cleaning to a different day or time. More often than not, the homeowner says yes. The housekeeper perceives the owner as easy going, and she's appreciative of being able to adjust her schedule when needed. The homeowner, however, perceives the housekeeper as erratic with scheduling and feels frustrated by the requests. The owner expects her to maintain a consistent schedule each week. You can see the assumptions, expectations and perceptions are creating a significant misunderstanding and rift in this relationship.

CONCLUSION

As you move beyond the challenges in this life, much like a sage, you will be standing more clearly in your own truth. All of the external influences that lead to telling others about them—and that define your assumptions, expectations and perceptions—will diminish or disappear. As you gain freedom from the need to look externally for acceptance or approval, your language and voice will become a language of YOUR truth that comes from YOUR voice.

You'll be less inclined to become defensive with Other. You'll also be less apt to hesitate, lie or avoid speaking your truth. You no longer will communicate to change Other; you're communicating to teach Other about YOU. In the process, this frees you to explore them. You know how important it is for you to be known and to move beyond those who think they know you. So, you offer that to Other. You offer them your interest in learning about them.

By having an internal frame of reference, you open your Self to be the observer of Self and Other. In that realm, you can see how the aforementioned aspects of communication can lead to miscommunication through learned and fear-based emotion or experiences. As you learn to communicate through exploring and teaching, you see the impact of telling, assuming, expecting, and perceiving—and how that limits and detracts from Other and Self. You are able to use your learned assumptions, expectations, and perceptions to disentangle some of the discord in your communication.

The Sage's Template™ uses communication to open you to life's expansiveness. As a significant tool for mastering your life, communication and language must take the shape of opening you to freedom not closing you with limits. If communication is going to be about you and the experience you wish to have, then it must begin with YOU. It must be you *speaking your truth*.

This new style of communicating is coming from YOU and is about you. Therefore, you must understand your Self, the experiences you are having, and the ones you wish to have. It is from that point of reference and awareness that you share your Self with Other. Ultimately, it's not about how they may or may not respond to your experience. It's about you expressing your truth on your behalf.

You are being heard. Others now have the opportunity to understand you as you know your Self. From there, it's about asking others who they are, what they are thinking, what they are experiencing, and how they are feeling. You've learned that you can use assumptions, expectations, and perceptions (the aspects that usually break down communication and relationships) to grow and expand your communication and relationships.

You now have a circle of communicating that begins and ends with you, while inviting Other to do the same. It's a style that can open you and your relationships to happiness. It's also one that will redefine your world as you begin to be present in life and with Other.

CHAPTER

8

Conclusion

This life is an experience. It's presented in a dualistic model. It's defined by challenges and truth, and it's understood from the perspectives of Self and Other. It's both physical and energetic. Free will exists in all aspects of life. Consequently, you are here to move through the dualistic experience and into the unity of The One by mastering the challenges, or fears, that create the illusion of being separate from Spirit or The One. You will choose to master these challenges partially, fully, or not at all. You can heal as much of the suffering as you choose.

You are here to "get in tune" with The One. The challenges in this life are those fears that create the illusion that you are out of tune with or separate from The One. Challenges are learned from Other when fears and rules are put upon you in a way that does not match your truth. Where you felt love and acceptance during your formative years, your truth grew. Where you felt put upon by expectations, assumptions, blame and more, you felt limited and learned fear. Your core challenges set the stage for the experience you are here to have.

The sage masters his/her challenges and seeks the inward journey that unveils truth and inner freedom. As you understand the experience of the sage, you can feel where you are headed in the mastery of this life. You are breaking free of the imposed limitations taught to you by Other—and unveiling your truth within.

The Sage's Template™ offers you a way to simplify the mastery by using the dualistic model of this life and guiding you through the transcendence of fears so that you are living in balance, centered in your truth. It suggests ways to heal your challenges by learning what is truly you and what belongs to Other. Once you have discerned the experiences, you are ready to heal the Self and shed the inflicted challenge.

You are always both a physical being and an energetic being. You're always in relationship with both and communicating with both. Therefore, it is through the knowing of both aspects of you that you begin to break free of the limitations of this life.

Through communication you learned the challenges, and through communication you can undo the challenges that prevent you from knowing your inner experience and speaking your truth. In turn, this allows you to teach Other who and what you are. It frees you of having to "try" to meet all external pressures and allows you to focus on you—what you are experiencing and what you wish to experience.

It's time to turn the page and begin a new chapter—one filled with truth, awareness, happiness, and wisdom.

Let The Sage's Template™ be your guide.

Appendix A

Fear-based emotions

Abandoned	Contempt	Disrespected	Ignored
Agitated	Controlled	Embarrassed	Impatient
Alienated	Controlling	Empty	Inadequate
Alone	Cranky	Envied	Indifferent
Angry	Cravings	Envious	Indignant
Angst	Criticized	Estranged	Insecure
Annihilated	Defeated	Fear	Insignificant
Annoyed	Defensive	Foolish	Insulted
Anxious	Demoralized	Forced	Irresponsible
Apathetic	Denial	Forlorn	Irritated
Appalled	Depressed	Frustrated	Isolated
Apprehensive	Desire	Fury	Invisible
Argumentative	Despair	Greedy	Jealous
Attached	Destroyed	Grief	Judged
Banished	Devalued	Guilty	Lazy
Betrayed	Disappointed	Hate	Less than
Bitter	Disappointing	Hated	Lonely
Bored	Discarded	Heartbroken	Loss
Chastised	Disempowered	Heartless	Lost
Cheated	Disgust	Helpless	Lusting
Combative	Disgusted	Hopeless	Malicious
Competitive	Disliked	Humiliated	Manipulated
Compulsive	Dismayed	Humiliating	Misunderstood
Confused	Disregarded	Hurt	Needy

Nonbelonging	Publicly shamed	Sad	Tense
Not Good Enough	Rage	Scared	Threatened
Objectified	Rejected	Scorned	Torn
Obsessive	Rejecting	Scorning	Uncomfortable
Oppressed	Remorseful	Self-Conscious	Unfair
Ostracized	Repressed	Self-Important	Unimportant
Outcast	Resented	Self-Pity	Unjust
Overwhelmed	Resentful	Selfishness	Unknown
Pain	Resistant	Separate	Used
Pained	Revengeful	Shame	Vain
Perfectionist	Revulsion	Shy	Violated
Persecuted	Righteous	Smothered	Vulnerable
Prideful	Righteously	Stubborn	Worthless
Procrastination	Indignant	Stupid	Worried

Printed in the United States
by Baker & Taylor Publisher Services